The Detroit News

RETURN TO ROSES

THE DRAMATIC STORY OF MSU'S ROAD TO THE 2013 BIG TEN CHAMPIONSHIP

KCI SPORTS PUBLISHING

Credits

The Detroit News

Editor & Publisher: Jonathan Wolman
Managing Editor: Gary Miles

Detroit News MSU Football Writer: Matt Charboneau
Detroit News columnists: Bob Wojnowski, John Niyo
Sports Editor: Phil Laciura
Photographer: Dale G. Young
Photo & Video Editor: John T. Greilick

Multimedia Editor: Pam Shermeyer

Book Editor and Designer: Richard Epps, *Presentation Editor*
Copy Editor: Craig Mantey

Read more of The Detroit News' Michigan State football stories at www.detroitnews.com

Peter J. Clark, Publisher
Molly Voorheis, Managing Editor
Nicky Brillowski, Book and Cover Design
Sam Schmidt, Advertising

ISBN: 978-1-940056-05-0 (HC)

Printed in the United States of America
KCI Sports Publishing   3340 Whiting Avenue, Suite 5   Stevens Point, WI 54481
Phone: 1-800-697-3756   Fax: 715-344-2668
www.kcisports.com

Contents

Foreword

Dantonio instilled belief in his team at last year's team banquet

By Matt Charboneau

When Michigan State closed 2012 with a 6-6 regular-season record, coach Mark Dantonio stood in front of his team at its annual banquet and told them they would be the next Michigan State team to go to the Rose Bowl.

It seemed far-fetched at the time, and at various points of the 2013 season, seemed just as improbable.

But Dantonio instilled a belief in his team very few shared and the results have been historic.

There were plenty of firsts in 2013, including the first 8-0 mark in Big Ten play, the first time the Spartans have won 12 games, and the first victory in the Big Ten championship game.

Fans of all ages reveled in Michigan State's historic football season.

Foreword

However the biggest accomplishment has been, without question, the team's first trip to the Rose Bowl in 26 years.

It was a difficult start to the season as the Spartans struggled to score points while relying on an outstanding defense. But by the time Big Ten play began, things started to turn, leading to one of the more memorable seasons in Michigan State history.

From the domination of Michigan to the program's first victory over Nebraska, to the Big Ten championship game triumph over Ohio State, it was remarkable.

As Michigan State tries to cap things in style in the Rose Bowl against Stanford, we go back and relive how it all happened – how Connor Cook seized the quarterback job, how Shilique Calhoun emerged as a defensive menace, how Jeremy Langford became one of the most productive runners in the Big Ten.

Those just scratch the surface of a season few Michigan State fans will forget.

Everyone on campus, even MSU basketball coach Tom Izzo,
cheered on the Spartans football team this season.

Spartan Stadium fans signal for a safety as Youngstown State starts with the ball deep in its own territory during the September 14 game in East Lansing.

The Spartan marching band performs during halftime of the Western Michigan game.

Max Bullough

Spartans lose their heart, soul with Bullough suspended for Rose Bowl

By Matt Charboneau

To attempt to quantify what Max Bullough means to the Michigan State football team – or more accurately now, what the team has lost – is nearly impossible.

There are plenty of impressive accolades. He's been All-Big Ten twice, is a third-team All-American this season, a two-time captain and an Academic All-American. He's also the leader of the No. 1 defense in the nation, orchestrating every aspect of the Spartans' attack from his middle linebacker position.

But now that the senior has been suspended for Michigan State's Rose Bowl matchup with Stanford for violating team rules, it is not a stretch to say the Spartans have lost their heart, lost their soul.

That's not a slight to the rest of the Spartans who have won 12 games this season, captured a Big Ten championship and earned the team's first Rose Bowl berth in 26 years. However, no

Max Bullough

player has meant more to this program than Bullough.

Few players can match Bullough's intensity or knowledge of the game, and quite frankly, his leadership has been unmatched. That makes his transgression – whatever it is – even more puzzling considering the state it has left his team heading into its biggest game in decades.

The player most would look to for leadership in working out of a difficult situation is Bullough, and now his teammates must regroup without him.

The Rose Bowl has been everything to Bullough. It's been ingrained in him since he was young, the grandson of Spartan great Hank Bullough and the son of former MSU lineback-er Shane Bullough. His uncles, Chuck Bullough and Bobby Morse, also played for the Spartans.

Being Michigan State's middle linebacker was in his blood and getting the Spartans back to the Rose Bowl was what pushed him every day – as a true freshman playing on special teams and backing up Greg Jones, to a junior imploring his team to beat Minnesota to become bowl-eligible in the final week of the 2012 season, and ultimately being the centerpiece of the best defense in the nation in 2013.

And now, with that dream of a Rose Bowl finally realized, Bullough didn't even make the trip.

"You're sitting at this point at the end of your senior year and you've gone through a lot," Bullough said last week. "You've done a lot of hard work, done a lot of good things.

"It's been great. It's been everything we ever dreamed of. Coming off that Big Ten championship game, it was an emotional win, it's a win that was huge for this program, but ultimately we need to play well and win the Rose Bowl, be Rose Bowl champions. Not only is that setting this team off right, it finishes the season the way we want to, on a positive note."

Any chance of that is gone for Bullough, and without their heart and soul, it has now become unbelievably difficult for the Spartans.

Mark Dantonio and the Spartan squad run onto the field as MSU visits Notre Dame.

Max Bullough

Locker-room speech sets the stage for memorable senior season

Just two days into his final preseason camp, linebacker Max Bullough stood in front of his teammates to deliver his senior speech.

It's a tradition at Michigan State. Some speeches go quickly, some last a bit longer, but they are all unique and personal to each player.

As Bullough talked, linebackers coach Mike Tressel was struck by what he was witnessing.

This wasn't just any player talking about his four years as a Spartan. This was a historian of the program, a coach, a player, all wrapped into one. It was, quite simply, unlike anything he has witnessed.

It was, as Tressel pointed out, the entire package.

"It was good as I've ever seen," Tressel said.

When Bullough's career ends after this season, his numbers won't say he's the best Michigan State has ever seen. At 223 career tackles, he'll likely end up just inside the top 20 in school history. His 111 tackles last season also don't crack the top 10 for a single season at Michigan State.

But those are the numbers, and they simply don't tell the entire story. The career tackles are lower, in part, because he played behind Greg Jones as a freshman. He's never had to put up gaudy single-season numbers because the entire de-

fense has been dominant.

Yet, when anyone around the program is asked, there is no hesitation as to how Bullough is perceived.

"I don't think you can replace the whole package that is Max Bullough," Tressel said. "Can you get another football player that is similar? Sure. Can you get another great kid? Absolutely. Can you get another leader? I don't know if you can get another leader like him, to be honest. But you have to put it all together and that's what's different about him."

And Michigan State has been the beneficiary the past three seasons.

The list of great Michigan State linebackers is long and includes the likes of Jones, Percy Snow and Dan Bass along with Max Bullough's father, Shane, and uncle, Chuck.

And Bullough belongs on the same level, even if the numbers don't quite measure up.

He has been a leader since the day he stepped on campus, last year's captain desig-

Max Bullough brings down the Purdue quarterback.

Max Bullough

Max Bullough forces the ball out of Indiana QB Nate Sudfeld's hands.

Max Bullough

Max Bullough carries on his family's proud tradition of Michigan State football.

Max Bullough

nation was merely a formality.

Bullough was asked recently what makes a good leader and little did he know he was describing himself. He used words like accountability, work and trust.

"I want to be part of the team that brings Michigan State back to the Rose Bowl," he said. "I want to get us back there, I want to get us back to that stature nationally. And I want to be remembered and argued as having the best defense in Michigan State history. I know you can argue about the 1960s and whatever, and it's kind of like arguing LeBron vs. Jordan; you'll never have a definitive answer. But I want to be in the argument. I want people to say when they're asked, 'What year was Michigan State's defense the best?' I want them to include these past four years."

It's no surprise Bullough is focused on the big picture. After all, there might not be a family that identifies itself with Michigan State more than the Bulloughs.

Max's grandfather, Hank, started it all by playing and coaching at Michigan State. His father, Shane, was next, racking up 311 tackles from 1983-86. Then came his uncle, Chuck, who has 391 career tackles and still holds the single-season mark with 175 in 1991. Younger brother Riley is a redshirt freshman and slated to be the starting running back this season and youngest brother, Byron, will be on campus next fall.

Max Bullough said it's "an honor" to follow in the family's footsteps and hopes he's honored them by being his own man.

"I look at it more as an opportunity than something that (is pressure)," he said. "As I played I created my own little legacy and that's what my family would want, to create a name for myself and I think I've done that,

not in spite of them but in honor of them."

Time catches up quick.

There is little doubt Bullough has exceeded in that category. Not only has he been outstanding on the field, he also will graduate in December with a degree in finance. And until he makes that next step in life — likely the NFL — he's going to try and appreciate his final season, even if it has gone far quicker than he would have ever imagined.

"It's something you don't realize until you're a senior," he said. "This is my last time around, this is my last chance, my last time to play Michigan, Nebraska, Notre Dame, whatever it is. I don't get to do it again and that's weird to me. For so much of my life I've been looking forward to playing at Michigan State and now I'm here. I've been looking forward to playing and all of a sudden I'm going to be looking back pretty soon. I've got to make the best out of this season and I know I'm in the midst of doing it."

And if Bullough has proven anything, making the best out of this season has little to do with whether anyone thinks he's the best linebacker to play at Michigan State.

Sure, he wants to be great and admits being an All-American would be pretty cool, and an academic All-American would be nice, too.

"But that comes with winning," he said. "If I do those things I think we're gonna be in the winning column as well."

It's about the whole package for him, and that's what makes Bullough one of the best.

MICHIGAN STATE **26** WESTERN MICHIGAN **13**

OMINOUS CLOUDS
OVER OFFENSE

Michigan State 26, Western Michigan 13

QB-receiver miscues have Spartans groping for answers

Friday, August 30, 2013 | East Lansing
Story by Matt Charboneau | Photos by Dale G. Young

East Lansing — For 13 games last season, Michigan State watched its offense flounder over and over while routinely hoping its defense would be good enough to make up the difference.

It was able to on most nights, but it was hardly enough as the Spartans struggled to finish 7-6 and didn't win a conference game at home.

Just one game into the 2013 season, things don't appear a whole lot different.

Michigan State won its season-opener at

Aaron Burbridge hauls in a reception for the Spartans.

Michigan State 26, Western Michigan 13

Spartan Stadium on Friday night, beating Western Michigan, 26-13, in front of 71,214 mostly rain-soaked fans.

And yes, the defense was outstanding, scoring two touchdowns — one more than the offense — turning the ball over four times and piling up five sacks.

But the offense was inept again, punting 11 times and turning the ball over once. The wide receivers, who contributed to more than 60 drops last season, dropped as many as six on Friday night and the quarterbacks — senior Andrew Maxwell and sophomore Connor Cook — were far from outstanding.

"You always worry when you don't see things come to fruition," coach Mark Dantonio said. "We have to deal with the current situation and deal with the present. What I've seen is we have caught the ball all summer long very, very well and for whatever reason, tonight we didn't catch the ball. We had too many drops. I didn't think our quarterback play was bad. There's gonna be plays you want back as a quarterback, but when the ball is on the money, you've got to make the catch. It's pretty simple."

Maxwell started the game and was 11-for-21 for 74 yards. Cook played nearly as much, going 6-for-16 for 42 yards while also running four times for 35 yards.

"I missed a couple throws tonight, and I certainly want to become more efficient,"

Connor Cook scrambles for yardage during the season opener.

Cook said. "I ran the ball well when the opportunity was there. I got too excited when guys were wide open, so the ball sailed on me. I didn't try to force any throws, and for the most part, I made good decisions."

But the bigger issue was, again, the drops. Senior Bennie Fowler contributed three

Michigan State 26, Western Michigan 13

*Linebacker Jairus Jones (23) dives for yardage after an interception as
safety Kurtis Drummond (27) looks on.*

of them, despite having a 26-yard catch on Michigan State's only touchdown drive of the game.

However, Fowler wasn't the only one to have issues as Aaron Burbridge and Keith Mumphery both dropped passes and seven different receivers got in the game. It was all very disheartening to Dantonio.

"I've seen them all make great catches," Dantonio said. "But you've got to come up with the tough catch sometimes. Quite frankly, there were a number of them that hit us

right square in the numbers that they've got to make. That's harsh, but that's life sometimes. I'm here to call it like I see it."

It was also far from what co-offensive co-ordinator Dave Warner was looking for in his first game running the offense.

"Very disappointing for us as an offensive football team, I think that's pretty obvious," he said. "We put a big emphasis, going all the way back to spring practice, on not making mistakes as far as the penalties, throwing and catching the ball with a high percentage,

Denicos Allen (28) makes life difficult for Western Michigan's quarterback.

Michigan State 26, Western Michigan 13

which we didn't do, and creating big plays, which we didn't do. Those were probably the three big things that stand out in my mind. Very disappointed."

What was somewhat lost in the poor night from the offense was another outstanding performance from the defense.

Jairus Jones, converted safety now playing linebacker in his final season, had two interceptions and his first led to the first score of the game.

After picking off a Tyler Van Tubbergen pass at the Western Michigan 24, Jones flipped the ball to safety Kurtis Drummond, who took it 22 yards for the score less than halfway through the first quarter. Drummond added a one-handed interception later in the first quarter, but the offense couldn't capitalize and was forced to punt.

Then the weather came in during the second quarter and led to a 56-minute delay.

When the teams returned, Michigan State was flat while Western Michigan took advantage. After Van Tubbergen connected with Timmy Keith for a 45-yard gain, the Broncos capitalized when backup quarterback Zach Terrell hit tight end Clark Mussman for a 14-yard touchdown to tie the game at 7.

But the Spartans bounced back with their only real efficient offensive drive of the game. A seven-play, 69-yard drive ended with a 2-yard touchdown run from Jeremy Langford, who finished with 94 yards on 20 carries.

A poor snap on the extra point left Michigan State ahead 13-7 at halftime.

In the second half, the Spartans added two field goals from Kevin Muma as Maxwell and Cook continued to rotate but neither could move the ball efficiently.

"It wasn't scripted," Dantonio said of the rotation. "I made the call on the quarterbacks. In the second half, we just moved them. We took the attitude that if you moved the football, you stayed in. If you don't move it, we use the other guy. That's something we've got to do sometimes. That's harsh, but the quarterback's job is to make good decisions, to lead, to create. ... I think both quarterbacks played well enough to generate more points than what we got from our offense."

The defense capped Michigan State's scoring in the fourth quarter when Shilique Calhoun picked up a fumble forced by Marcus Rush and ran 16 yards for the touchdown with just more than nine minutes left in the game.

Rush finished with two sacks while Max Bullough had nine tackles and the Spartans racked up nine tackles-for-loss.

"Obviously, the thing to talk about here is the defense," Dantonio said. "I thought they played extremely well. I think they had maybe two first downs or three until the last series on third down conversions. Those are positives. We need to dwell on those positives and build on them. We need to always play to our strengths, period."

Western Michigan added a touchdown with 1:51 to play in the game when Terrell hit Corey Davis for a 14-yard touchdown pass. Terrell finished 12-for-28 for 120 yards.

"At the end of the day, the goal is to win and we got a win," Dantonio said. "From that standpoint, goal number one accomplished, but what we've got to do is clean up things."

DEFENSE
MECHANISM

Michigan State 21, South Florida 6

Defense dazzles, but MSU definitely concerned about offense

Saturday, September 7, 2013 | East Lansing
Story by Matt Charboneau | Photos by Dale G. Young

East Lansing — Michigan State coach Mark Dantonio was quick to point out late Saturday afternoon that things could always be worse.

He was right about that. His team did improve to 2-0 with a 21-6 victory over South Florida at Spartan Stadium. And, as he said, when compared to losing 9-7, that isn't all that bad.

But that's a fairly simplistic look at what has transpired over the first two weeks of the season.

While the Spartans have been dominant on defense, scoring four touchdowns in two weeks and creating six turnovers, the offense has been anything but dominating. In fact, it has been close to awful.

As Dantonio said, the running game was OK, but the passing game continues to be a significant problem. Sophomore Connor

Bennie Fowler (13) hauls in a pass for MSU.

Michigan State 21, South Florida 6

Denicos Allen (28) and Isaiah Lewis (9) bring down a South Florida runner.

Cook started at quarterback but also split time with red-shirt freshman Tyler O'Connor and senior Andrew Maxwell.

None of the three was especially effective and they combined for just 94 yards passing for an offense that generated just one touchdown for the second straight week.

"Of course I'm concerned," Dantonio said. "On a scale of 1 to 10? You know, if you were the head coach, I'd say it's about 8. Is that good enough? I'm concerned. We need explosive plays in our offense. (We) got the ball too many times in positions what I would consider sudden-change, and we're not generating points."

Much like the opener, the defense was the source of most of the scoring.

With the game scoreless midway through the second quarter, Tyler Hoover sacked South Florida quarterback Bobby Eveld and forced a fumble. Shilique Calhoun up scooped the ball and ran 4 yards for the touchdown to give Michigan State a 7-0 lead.

After South Florida got a pair of field goals from Marvin Kloss to make it 7-6 at halftime, Calhoun struck again.

Midway through the third quarter, Denicos Allen hit Eveld as he threw and the ball fluttered through the air. Calhoun snatched it out of the air and returned it 56 yards for the touchdown and a 14-6 lead.

"Shilique, he's our running back on defense, I guess you hand it off to him and let him go," defensive coordinator Pat Narduzzi said. "He's a great player, we knew he was a great player. There's a difference between hav-

Michigan State 21, South Florida 6

Riley Bullough plows through a gaping hole cleared by the MSU offensive line.

Michigan State 21, South Florida 6

ing a guy that makes plays in practice, and the guy that makes plays in the game and catches it and finishes it, so it's good to see."

Those types of plays continue to be lacking, however, on the offensive side of the ball.

Cook, who finished 6-for-11 for 32 yards, couldn't get the offense moving in the first half, giving way to O'Connor in the second quarter. He got the Spartans inside the South Florida 5-yard line but nearly threw an interception in the end zone on third down. The drive ended with Kevin Muma missing a 25-yard field goal.

O'Connor did not play again the rest of the game and to start the second half, Maxwell got the call. He was 4-for-9 for 40 yards but the offense still had trouble moving.

"Guys are getting opportunities, no two ways about it," offensive coordinator Dave Warner said. "The bottom line about those guys — I think I said it last week — is going to be who puts us in the end zone. Again, we had a field goal opportunity that was missed. We can't settle for field goals when we're first-and-goal. We can't settle for field goals. We went through that last year. Again, emphasis was made throughout the last seven months and we didn't get it done today as far as scoring in the red zone in that situation."

The Spartans got a bit of a spark at times from the running game. Nick Hill carried nine times for 63 yards, including a 23-yarder, while Riley Bullough had a 19-yard gain while picking up 36 for the game.

But it provided little solace for an offense that was outscored by its own defense for the second straight game.

And it did little to appease the crowd, which sat through a weather delay of more than an hour before the game and showered

the team with boos on the way to the locker room.

Dantonio shared their frustration.

"It doesn't bother me," Dantonio said of the crowd's reaction. "I wish, I guess, they weren't booing, but I understand where they're at. I'm just trying to stay positive. I think it's important we stay positive and reinforce it to our players."

Youngstown State comes to town next week with a trip to Notre Dame the following week.

While Dantonio doesn't believe the offense is under some sort of a deadline to work out its issues, he does understand things must improve.

"There's a sense of urgency because we want to be the best," Dantonio said. "I think we have a championship defense, I think we can do things on special teams to a championship level and we have to raise our performance on offense, cause we're not shooting for 7-6.

"But again, I'll go back to what I said initially: We have great chemistry here, a great family, support within our football team and because of that we'll get better. We'll push it through. We just need a spark to ignite the flame. We've got guys that can catch the football. We've got guys who can throw the football. The timing just has to come forward. We just need a spark. We need a couple guys to make a play."

MSU backup QB Tyler O'Connor yells out signals at the line of scrimmage. ▶

Michigan State 21, South Florida 6

QUESTIONS
ANSWERED

Michigan State 55, Youngstown State 17

Cook answers Michigan State QB question in rout of Youngstown State

Saturday, September 14, 2013 | East Lansing
Story by Matt Charboneau | Photos by Dale G. Young

East Lansing — Michigan State discovered its offense on Saturday, and in the process, it appears it has solved the massive question of who will be the starting quarterback.

Connor Cook was 15-for-22 for 202 yards and threw four touchdown passes to lead Michigan State (3-0) to a 55-17 victory over Youngstown State in front of 71,626 fans at Spartan Stadium.

"I thought Connor played well," Michigan State coach Mark Dantonio said. "It was our plan to go with him and stick with him a little bit even if he had a difficult time. I thought he responded.

"Connor Cook is the No. 1 quarterback. He's the No. 1 guy."

Jack Allen (66) and Jack Conklin (74) clear a running lane for Riley Bullough.

Michigan State 55, Youngstown State 17

Jeremy Langford turns the corner and outraces a defender.

It was quite the statement for a player in just his second start and caught in the thick of a heated quarterback battle.

Cook got the bulk of the work with the first team throughout the week while redshirt freshman Tyler O'Connor and Damion Terry also saw work with the first team. But by late in the week, Dantonio was confident Cook would be the guy he was planning to go with.

"He's always been a good practice player," Dantonio said of Cook. "I think all of our guys work hard out there. He had a very good Thursday practice. I really thought he threw the ball well on Thursday. We upped the tempo on things on how he was handling the huddle and that was a positive."

Cook said he knew early in the week he was going to get a shot to play, and not just

Michigan State 55, Youngstown State 17

Ezra Robinson (37) brings down a Youngstown State ballcarrier.

Michigan State 55, Youngstown State 17

for a few series. The fact he was going to get extended playing time made a big difference, he said, in his performance.

"When I sat down with coach Dantonio, he said, 'You're the guy and we believe in you, we have all the confidence in the world with you,' " Cook said. "I talked with some other people and they said the same stuff. It is just reassuring. I think I found my rhythm pretty early tonight, just like the last couple games. It's hard to find a rhythm when you are working with two other QBs or another QB."

Cook made it clear very early another quarterback would not be needed on this day. He led the Spartans to a touchdown on each of their first three drives, beginning with a 3-yard run from Jeremy Langford, followed by a 13-yard pass to Andre Sims Jr. and a 12-yard pass to fullback Trevon Pendleton, who found himself wide open in the end zone.

After Youngstown State took advantage of a fumbled punt by Sims to cut the lead to 21-10 on a 5-yard run by Martin Ruiz, Cook displayed what might have been his best throw of the game.

And it came on a drive that lasted only one play.

After Shilique Calhoun recovered a fumble for the third straight game, Cook threw a strike to Macgarrett Kings Jr., who went up and grabbed the ball as two defenders closed in and put the Spartans ahead 28-10.

"He catches everything," Dantonio said of Kings, who got his first start last week. "His confidence is very high right now and that's what you do. You put a premium on confidence when you're a skill player, whether that's the quarterback, tailback, or wideout. When your confidence is high, you can catch it all."

Cook added a 17-yard touchdown pass to Bennie Fowler to close out the second quarter and give the Spartans a 35-10 lead at halftime.

"I thought I did a lot better than the first two weeks," Cook said. "Guys were making plays, I was getting it to Macgarrett, he was making plays and I got it to Bennie, too. I was throwing a simple hitch route and it turned into a touchdown. Trevon was making plays. I don't know how many guys I hit, but I felt like I was getting a lot of guys involved. When you have that many guys involved in the offense, it's going to be dangerous."

Cook became the first Michigan State quarterback to throw for four touchdowns in a game since Brian Hoyer in 2007 and the first to do it in one half since Drew Stanton did it against Illinois in 2005.

He led one more scoring drive to open the second half, a quick, six-play drive that was mostly Nick Hill. The junior running back carried the ball five times and capped things off with a 35-yard touchdown run to put the Spartans ahead 42-10.

Cook's day was done at that point and redshirt freshman Tyler O'Connor came on. He played well, also, going 7-for-10 while helping Michigan State add another 13 points. Langford added another touchdown run and Kevin Muma kicked a pair of field goals.

"There's no substitute for that game experience and obviously I had a lot of it today because the first-team offense performed so well in the first half," O'Connor said. "It's great to get out there and really get into the rhythm basically for a full half. We moved the ball and did some good things, so I feel pretty good about today."

Youngstown State (2-1) got one more score from Ruiz, this time on a 34-yard catch, to cut the deficit some, but this day was about

Michigan State 55, Youngstown State 17

Connor Cook (18) and Shilique Calhoun (89) lead a postgame celebration.

Cook and the Michigan State offense.

It came later than some had hoped, but heading to Notre Dame next week, the Michigan State offense has its quarterback.

"I think you want to make decisions as soon as you can, but sometimes I don't make that decision, the players make that decision," Dantonio said. "They have to play well under some pressure situations and continue to play well. When it's close and you're going back and forth, you sort of have to let things roll as a coach."

Dantonio did that and Cook did just what his coach has been asking for by seizing the opportunity.

OUT OF
REACH

Notre Dame 17, Michigan State 13

Missed chances cost Michigan State in loss to Notre Dame

Saturday, September 21, 2013 | South Bend, Indiana
Story by Matt Charboneau | Photos by Dale G. Young

South Bend, Ind. — There were questionable penalty calls, even more questionable play calls, and plenty of missed opportunities.

It was hardly what Michigan State was looking for Saturday at Notre Dame Stadium, and in the end it proved too much to overcome as Notre Dame held on for a 17-13 victory as the Spartans head into a bye week.

"It's hard," senior linebacker Max Bullough said. "They respect you and you respect them. It's tough to sit and take a loss, especially in an away stadium just because it's that much louder and that much more in your face. It's tough, but we'll get over it and move forward."

The penalties hurt. The lack of touchdowns in the red zone did, as well. But the bottom line is Michigan State (3-1) is still an outstanding defensive football team with an offense that is far from competent.

Three straight times in the fourth quarter, with Notre Dame clinging to a four-point lead,

Micajah Reynolds, left, and Marcus Rush shut down an Irish ballcarrier.

Notre Dame 17, Michigan State 13

Coach Mark Dantonio shows his frustration during MSU's only regular-season loss.

the Michigan State defense forced Notre Dame to go three plays and out. But three straight times the offense did absolutely nothing.

The Spartans defense was outstanding again, allowing just 224 total yards. The running game was also efficient, gaining 119 yards against one of the better run defenses in the country.

"Last year against Notre Dame I felt like we were completely outplayed," Michigan State coach Mark Dantonio said. "I felt like

this time we were right down to the end. I thought we competed and played right through it. There was a lot of emotion on our sidelines. We played to win.

"But at the end of the day they do keep score. So we got to deal with it. That's part of growing up. That's part of trying to be mature about everything we deal with. In the end it will help us."

It didn't take long for Michigan State to make something happen, but it also didn't take long for the offense to come up short.

Notre Dame 17, Michigan State 13

Macgarrett Kings Jr. races downfield for additional yardage.

After forcing the Irish to go three-and-out on their first possession, Matt Macksood blocked the Notre Dame punt and Michigan State took over at the Notre Dame 31.

However, after picking up just one first down, the drive stalled and Kevin Muma was called on to kick a 30-yard field goal. He pulled it wide and didn't see the field again other than to kick off.

Notre Dame was first to get on the board late in the first quarter with a 41-yard field goal from Kyle Brindza, but the drive was an indication of how things would go for much of the game. With Notre Dame facing a third-and-9 from its 21, Darqueze Dennard was called for defensive holding. The drive continued and the Irish eventually took the 3-0 lead.

Michigan State did take advantage of a missed Brindza field goal early in the second quarter and marched 79 yards on 14 plays

Notre Dame 17, Michigan State 13

to take a 7-3 lead on a 12-yard touchdown pass from Connor Cook to Macgarrett Kings Jr. The Spartans' drive was aided by a pair of face-mask penalties on the Irish.

After the teams traded punts, Notre Dame got a short field and another call, the first of four pass interference penalties, and took a 10-7 lead into halftime.

The Spartans opened the second half with one of their best drives, marching all the way to the Notre Dame 8. But another touchdown opportunity was missed and they settled for a 25-yard field goal from Michael Geiger, the first of the freshman's career.

"Get down in the red zone, you got to score touchdowns," Dantonio said. "Had our opportunities in the red zone, kicked a couple field goals, missed one. You got to score

Shilique Calhoun (89) comes up with the ball for MSU.

Notre Dame 17, Michigan State 13

touchdowns in those situations."

With the running game rolling behind the play of Jeremy Langford, Michigan State called a reverse pass and put the ball in the hands of freshman R.J. Shelton. The play was supposed to go to Bennie Fowler, who had three Notre Dame defenders around him. Shelton threw it anyway and the ball was intercepted by Matthias Farley.

"I made the suggestion on that one because I felt like we needed a big play," Dantonio said. "He's got a great arm on him. The guy was covered. Probably should have just pulled it down and ran. So that's my call. I'll take responsibility for that. But I felt like we needed a big play."

Notre Dame got the ball at the Michigan State 37 after the Spartans were flagged for a late hit on the turnover, picked up two first downs on two more pass interference calls — one on Waynes and one on Dennard — and scored what would turn out to be the winner on a 7-yard run by Cam McDaniel.

Michigan State came right back on its next drive and had a first down at the Notre Dame 14. But a 5-yard loss and two penalties pushed the Spartans back and forced a 42-yard field goal from Geiger. Michigan State got three more possessions but never got past the 50-yard line as the offense could find little production through the air.

Cook finished 16-for-32 and was replaced by Andrew Maxwell on the final drive. Rees fared marginally better for the Irish, going 14-for-34 for 142 yards.

"I think both defenses really carried the day here today," Notre Dame coach Brian Kelly said. "I think Michigan State has a great defense. They're very difficult to play against in so many fashions. I think (Dennard) is probably one of the best corners that we've gone against, and I've seen them all. They're just a very difficult defense.

"If you would have asked me last week about what this kind of game was going to be, it wasn't going to be a beauty contest. I felt like it was going to be this kind of game."

The kind of game Michigan State has seen far too often.

Center Blake Treadwell (64) protects QB Connor Cook.

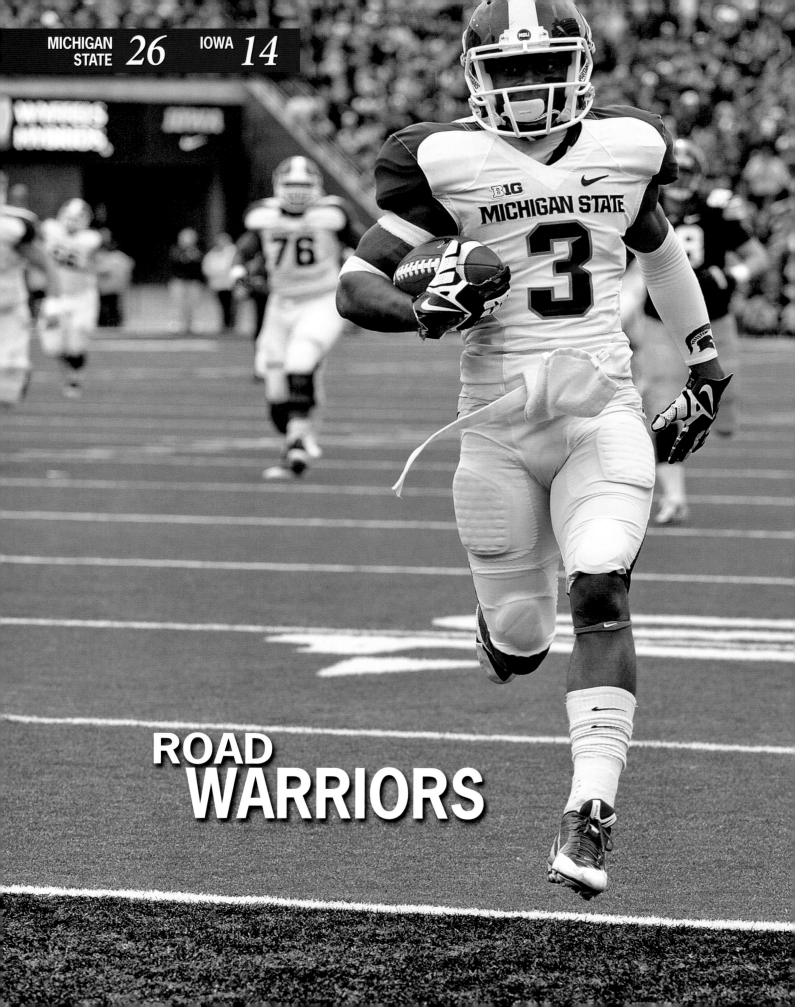

MICHIGAN STATE **26** IOWA **14**

ROAD
WARRIORS

Michigan State 26, Iowa 14

Michigan State offense catches on, wins Big Ten opener at Iowa

Saturday, October 5, 2013 | Iowa City, Iowa
Story by Matt Charboneau | Photos by Dale G. Young

Iowa City, Iowa — It's hard to put too much on the first conference game of the season, but Michigan State coach Mark Dantonio knew how important Saturday's matchup with Iowa was.

The Spartans have one of the best defenses in the nation, but their offense has been largely ineffective and they were coming off a disappointing loss two weeks ago at Notre Dame followed by a bye week. Add in the fact a Big Ten division loss would have put Michigan State behind right out of the gate and what it did at Kinnick Stadium was all the more impressive.

It can hardly be described as an offensive explosion, but for Michigan State, it was long overdue as it rolled up 412 total yards and quarterback Connor Cook threw for 277 yards and two touchdowns. The result was a 26-14 victory in front of a crowd of 69,025 that ended Iowa's four-game winning streak.

"This is a program win," Dantonio said Saturday afternoon. "We would have been 3-2 (with a loss), so everything is positive going forward. No, we haven't played our best football yet, but we've played really well at times and we're coming. We needed to look from within our team and find ourselves and

Darqueze Dennard is congratulated after the victory.

Michigan State 26, Iowa 14

I think we did that today."

What they found was an offense that proved as effective as it has been all season, something that no doubt was a welcome sight for a defense that came in ranked No. 1 in the country.

Senior Bennie Fowler, benched after the first game of the season, had a career-high nine catches for 92 yards, including a 37-yard touchdown grab. Sophomore Macgarrett Kings Jr. continued to shine, making five grabs for 94 yards and scoring on a 46-yard strike from Cook. The Spartans also got solid play from receiver Aaron Burbridge, and Tony Lippett had an outstanding first-down catch, as well.

"Our skill at wide receiver is pretty good," Dantonio said. "I know it hasn't been as consistent as we want, but the skill set you saw today with our guys making catches. Those guys are on the field to make plays."

It's been quite the change for a group that has been the focus of the offense's problems dating to last season. Drops have been frequent while big plays have been just the opposite.

That changed Saturday.

Kings made several nice moves on his touchdown and benefited from a block by Fowler. On another play Fowler earned a first down on sheer will, breaking a tackle and taking it up the sideline. And Lippett's first-down

MSU QB Connor Cook celebrates with his father after the victory.

grab early in the game was as good as it gets.

"Everyone is catching the ball great," Kings said. "We talk about it all the time and have a chip on our shoulder. We never forget the criticism and what everybody is saying about us. We use it as fuel to continue to do great things in the game."

There is no doubt the offense also was aided by Cook's best game.

He has struggled with his accuracy this season but was 25-for-44 on Saturday and

Michigan State 26, Iowa 14

Paul Lang (83) and Kodi Kieler (79) clear the way for for Mike Sadler (3).

Michigan State 26, Iowa 14

Jeremy Langford avoids an Iowa defender.

never looked out of sorts at any point.

"I was just loose," Cook explained. "Notre Dame was my first road start so I was a little uptight, but I came out today with a more loose mind-set and more confident."

It showed early as Michigan State got inside the Iowa 30 on three of its first four drives. However, the Spartans had only a 27-yard Michael Geiger field goal to show for it.

But the Spartans were moving the ball,

and Cook eventually connected with Kings to put Michigan State up 10-0 with 6:18 to play in the first half.

But Iowa (4-2, 1-1) showed it wasn't about to lie down on its home field.

The Hawkeyes gained 140 total yards on their final two drives of the first half, gaining just 20 in their other possessions. They cut a 10-0 Spartans lead to 10-7 on a 47-yard pass from Jake Rudock to Damon Bullock and

Michigan State 26, Iowa 14

went ahead on a 10-yard strike from Rudock to tight end C.J. Fiedorowicz. Before that, Iowa had not picked up a first down.

The problem for Iowa was Michigan State's offense took control at the outset of the second half, marching 75 yards on seven plays and finishing the drive with Fowler's touchdown.

Michigan State's defense clamped down and allowed Iowa only 23 rushing yards. The Hawkeyes also had 10 possessions that lasted three plays or fewer, including two that ended with interceptions.

"Our defense helped us out," Dantonio said. "They usually do."

Geiger added a 35-yard field goal late in third quarter to extend the lead to 20-14, and after another three-and-out, the Spartans got

tricky. Punter Mike Sadler ran for 25 yards on fourth-and-7 from the Michigan State 37 on the first play of the fourth quarter. Geiger nailed a career-best 49-yard field goal four plays later to extend the lead to 23-14.

The Spartans essentially put the game away with 5:25 to play on Geiger's fourth field goal, this time from 40 yards, as the defense closed the deal.

"This is a big team win," Dantonio said. "We've been thinking about our last game and how to strengthen ourselves and re-evaluating ourselves as a football team. We kept talking about how you're going to have to play through adversity and we just have to basically storm the gates. I just thought it was a great team win for our football team and we saw some outstanding things."

Connor Cook (18) and Tres Barksdale (87) lead a postgame victory celebration.

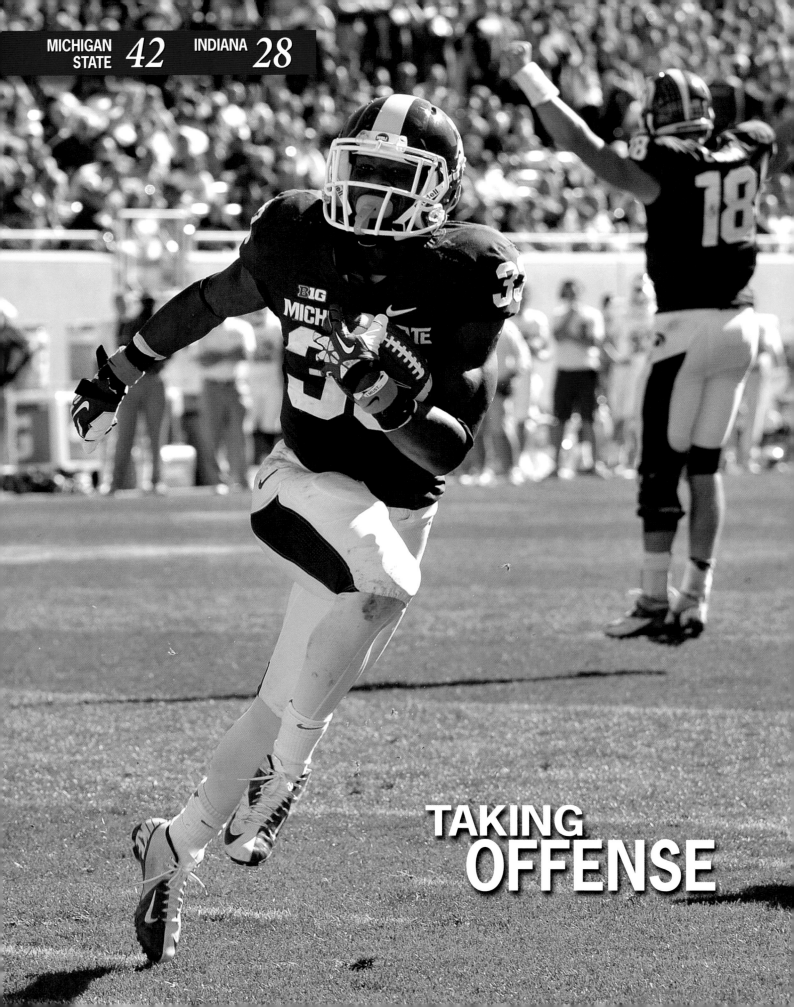

TAKING
OFFENSE

Michigan State 42, Indiana 28

Michigan State romps over Indiana in Big Ten home opener

Saturday, October 12, 2013 | East Lansing
Story by David Goricki | Photos by Dale G. Young

East Lansing — If there was any doubt the Spartans have found their quarterback in Connor Cook, he erased it Saturday.

Cook, a sophomore, led the Spartans on five straight scoring drives to help Michigan State to a 42-28 victory over Indiana Saturday afternoon, the 500th game played at Spartan Stadium.

MSU (5-1, 2-0 Big Ten) piled up 473 total yards against the Big Ten's worst defense, sending the 73,815 fans home happy on Homecoming.

How good was MSU's offense? After going three-and-out on their first two drives, the Spartans scored on their final three of the first half to take a 21-14 halftime lead. Then, they scored on their first two of the second half to open a 35-21 third-quarter lead.

"You've got to give a lot of credit to our offense in terms of what they were able to do, running the football, big plays in the passing game, explosive plays," MSU coach Mark Dantonio said. "I thought it was tremendous that we scored when we were in the red zone (3-for-3) today and had explosive plays. We have different guys making plays and that's what's so exciting for me.

Tyler Hoover puts the clamps on an Indiana ballcarrier.

Michigan State 42, Indiana 28

"Connor Cook played another solid game so good things are happening. Overall it's a great team win for us. We're 5-and-1. We can set the tone for the next phase; halfway through the season, now we start playing for things."

Dantonio is excited, too, with Cook running the offense. He completed 22 of 31 passes for 235 yards and two TDs. He had one interception, which bounced off a receiver's hand.

"Connor Cook is growing with confidence," Dantonio said. "He can make plays. He has a good arm. He's finding receivers and throws a very catchable football."

The Spartans were 7-of-9 on third-down conversions in the first half, then converted three straight to start the third quarter to open a 35-21 lead. They finished 10-of-14.

"I knew we were succeeding and converting on third downs," Cook said. "Coach (co-offensive coordinator Dave) Warner did a great job of calling plays, putting us in situations that we were in, going up against the right coverage with those plays.

Tight end Josiah Price (82) puts a stiff-arm on an Indiana defender.

"We heard what everyone's been saying all year long (criticizing MSU's offense) and we made it personal this week. We took it upon ourselves, as a team, as a unit. We talked about it earlier in the week and made it personal."

Cook completed three third-down passes on the first scoring drive, including an 11-yard TD pass to Jeremy Langford to pull the

Michigan State 42, Indiana 28

Spartans even at 7 with 13:34 left in the first half.

Cook's 34-yard TD pass to Bennie Fowler came on a third-down play midway through the second quarter to give the Spartans a 14-7 lead.

Then Cook did some damage with his arm and legs during a 14-play, 75-yard drive which ended on Langford's 5-yard run for a 21-14 lead with 37 seconds left in the half.

Cook found Tony Lippett on a third-down pass to the Indiana 49 when he rolled right and found his receiver over the middle. On a third-and-1 play, Cook ran for 8 yards to the Indiana 22, then found Lippett again on third down to the 5, setting up Langford's score.

Langford scored his third TD on a 2-yard run with 10:03 left in the third with the score set up by Cook's 39-yard pass to wide open tight end Josiah Price on third down. He then scored his fourth TD on a 32-yard run ...

again on third down, breaking a tackle at the line of scrimmage and sprinting down the left sideline for a 35-21 cushion with 3:23 left in the quarter.

So, why is Cook playing better now? He threw for 277 yards and 2 TDs in last week's 26-14 win at Iowa.

"I feel like I'm doing a better job of trusting my offensive line, waiting for the routes to develop," Cook said. "I'm waiting for things to develop."

It also helps that MSU had its running game going. Langford, a junior, rushed for 109 yards on 23 carries and scored those four TDs. Freshman Delton Williams gained 92 yards on 12 carries and freshman R.J. Shelton busted loose for a 34-yard TD.

MSU's defense did its job once again, too. The Spartans, ranked No. 1 in the nation in total defense, went up against the Big Ten's No. 1 offense, averaging 535 yards a game.

Freshman running back R.J. Shelton dives for extra yardage.

Michigan State 42, Indiana 28

Quarterback Connor Cook completed 22 of 31 passes for 235 yards against the Hoosiers.

Michigan State 42, Indiana 28

Delton Williams (22) outruns an Indiana defender.

They limited the Hoosiers' fast-paced style to 351.

The Hoosiers hit quickly with Tevin Coleman busting loose for a 64-yard TD run on the game's opening series. They scored a pair of TDs off MSU turnovers, a fumbled punt and the interception.

Indiana also had its chances after Coleman's TD, advancing into MSU territory on their next two series, then again when receiver Duwyee Wilson was wide open near midfield early in the second quarter, but Sudfeld threw it behind him after scrambling on a third-down play.

Sudfeld, who entered the game as the Big Ten's leader in total offense, was limited to 14-of-30 passing for 137 yards.

Still, the story was MSU's offense.

"It's almost more fun to watch them succeed as it is the defense in the past weeks," MSU senior linebacker Max Bullough said. "They've grown up so much and the young players have done so well, accepted the coaching. No one is talking bad about the Michigan State Spartans' offense anymore."

MICHIGAN STATE **14** PURDUE **0**

DEFENSE
NEVER
RESTS

Michigan State 42, Purdue 0

Offense sputters, but Michigan State prevails over Purdue

Saturday, October 19, 2013 | East Lansing
Story by Matt Charboneau | Photos by Dale G. Young

East Lansing — For the past two weeks, all the talk surrounding Michigan State's struggling offense had subsided.

The Spartans won two straight to open Big Ten play and did so behind an offense that was suddenly finding its way, making big plays and seeing its passing attack grow exponentially from the way it played in the nonconference season.

Connor Cook was getting comfortable as the Spartans' starting quarterback and the receivers were playing as well as they had since before last season. On top of that, the running game, which had been solid all season, was rolling along and the offensive line was playing outstanding.

It seemed the production would only continue Saturday with Purdue in town to face the Spartans. But as the old cliché goes, that's why they play the game.

And that's why Michigan State had to revert to its old formula — rely on its defense.

Tight end Andrew Gleichert (92) hauls in a touchdown pass from wide receiver Tony Lippett.

Michigan State 42, Purdue 0

Shilique Calhoun celebrates after a big defensive stop.

It did just that in a 14-0 victory over Purdue in front of an announced crowd of 71,514 at Spartan Stadium as linebacker Denicos Allen returned a fumble 45 yards for a touchdown in the second quarter to spark the victory. It was the only score of the game until Michigan State — which didn't get inside the Purdue 38-yard line until the fourth quarter — was able to put together its first solid offensive drive, icing the game on a 5-yard touchdown pass from wide receiver Tony Lippett to tight end Andrew Gleichert on a reverse pass.

"Well, we won the football game and I'm never going to apologize for winning," coach Mark Dantonio said. "It's a step forward. It's not a step back. A step back is when you lose. It's a step forward. There are plenty of people that take a step back and usually have an 'L' beside it.

"So we're 6-1. You can cut it anyway you want. We can sit there and say, we're not in the Top 25. We can moan and groan about it, or we can stay focused and do something about it."

Michigan State 42, Purdue 0

The win keeps Michigan State (6-1, 3-0 Big Ten) atop the Legends Division and made the Spartans bowl eligible, something they didn't achieve until the final game of the regular season last year.

But this team has much higher expectations, which made the offense's play all the more disappointing. Cook finished just 13-for-25 for 107 yards, but entering the final two drives of the game, he had thrown for only 33 yards and appeared on the verge of being lifted from the game.

Before Michigan State's nine-play touchdown drive, backup Tyler O'Connor was warming up on the sidelines and taking snaps from center Travis Jackson. Dantonio admitted he considered making the move, but decided to ride Cook for another series.

"There was a little bit of thought, I'll be honest with everybody, because as we move forward you have to win the football game," Dantonio said. "I wanted to stay with Connor Cook. I forced that issue a little bit. You never say never, I think that's just part of competition.

"He played well that last series. We kept him in and he played well. He took us down the field and scored, which was big. When you come in fresh off the sideline, it's difficult. We've been down that road before."

The decision to stick with Cook paid off with the score as he connected on passes of 18, 25 and 26 yards.

"I wasn't really stepping into my throws and I could have been a lot more accurate," Cook said. "The best thing is we finished strong, came together as a group at the end

Linebacker Taiwan Jones (34) slows down the Purdue rushing attack.

Michigan State 42, Purdue 0

and ran the ball great the whole game. Our offensive line — no surprise — did another amazing job and have been doing a great job all season long. We came together and finished strong, that's what matters."

It also matters that Cook feels far different than he did against Notre Dame when Andrew Maxwell came on for the final drive.

"I saw (O'Connor) warming up and stuff," Cook said. "But I know it means the coaches believe in me and they continue to believe I'm the guy and have faith in me. So that reassures me."

While Cook might be reassured, the offense's performance — at least in the passing game — can't be reassuring to many.

"It was very disappointing," offensive coordinator Dave Warner said. "We talked all week about not being satisfied with a couple good performances and the need to take it to the next level and step forward and we didn't do that today. We'll keep working on it, we'll be OK."

As much as the passing game struggled, the running game continued to be a strength for the Spar tans. Jeremy Langford carried 24 times for a career-best 131 yards, the second straight game he's gone over 100 yards.

Tyler Hoover (91) slows down the Purdue quarterback.

And the defense was outstanding in the second half, allowing just three first downs after giving up 11 in the first half. The Spartans allowed just 66 yards on the ground and held the Boilermakers (1-6, 0-3) to 226 total yards, including minus-5 yards in the fourth quarter.

"We haven't been able to finish drives all season long, and that was the case again today," Purdue coach Darrell Hazell said. "We'd get a penalty or a loss-yardage play on first down and then all of a sudden, we're second-and-12, second-and-13, and it's hard to overcome some of those as a young football team right now. But we need to be able to fin-

Michigan State 42, Purdue 0

ish those drives better."

Michigan State heads to Illinois next week with a chance to head into a difficult November in the driver's seat in the Legends.

"Hopefully, our football team is maturing as we move forward," Dantonio said. "We're understanding that nothing is easy and we mature and we grow. With every game we grow. That doesn't mean we're always going to have success, but we grow with that. That's reality and if you're able to do that, you're going to have a good football team."

Max Bullough (40) crunches Purdue's quarterback.

ALMOST
PERFECT

Michigan State 42, Illinois 3

Michigan State offense, defense dominate Illinois

Saturday, October 26, 2013 | Champaign, Ill.
Story by Matt Charboneau | Photos by Dale G. Young

Tight end Jamal Lyles eludes an Illinois defender.

Michigan State 42, Illinois 3

Champaign, Ill. — A week ago, some were wondering if Michigan State had taken a step in the wrong direction.

Its defense was typically solid in a win over Purdue, but the offense struggled — in particular, the passing game — and the Spartans managed just one offensive touchdown against one of the worst defenses in the Big Ten.

One week later, all of those concerns seem to be a distant memory.

Quarterback Connor Cook set a Michigan State completion-percentage record, completing 15 of 16 passes for 208 yards and three touchdowns to lead the Spartans (7-1, 4-0 Big Ten) to a dominating, 42-3 victory Saturday over Illinois in front of a homecoming crowd of 45,895 at Memorial Stadium.

It was the sixth-best completion percentage in Big Ten history and Cook finished the game with 11 straight completions, but it was just a single aspect of one of Michigan State's most complete performances in a long time. The Spartans rushed for 269 yards with Jeremy Langford carrying 22 times for 104 yards and

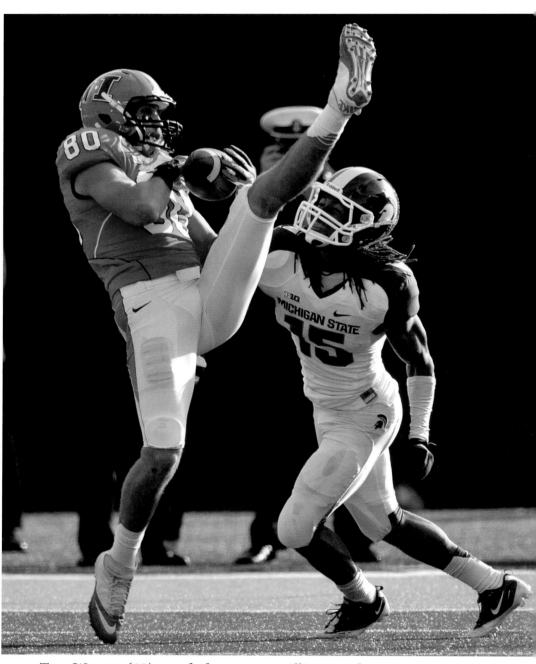

Trae Waynes (15) wreaks havoc on an Illinois wide receiver.

a pair of touchdowns, his third straight game going over the 100-yard mark.

And rarely lost in any Michigan State game is the play of the defense. Saturday was no different as the Spartans held Illinois (3-4, 0-3) to just 128 total yards, well below its

Michigan State 42, Illinois 3

average of 446.2 yards a game. Michigan State also held Illinois to 25 yards rushing and one first down in the second half.

"Outstanding job by our football team," coach Mark Dantonio said. "Great job by our defense; obviously in the second half we played very, very well. Cook obviously played very well and spread the ball around when we did throw it and involved three running

backs. I thought all three did an excellent job, and obviously it means our offensive line is playing well."

But the focus on this one has to be the play of the offense that managed 112 yards passing in the victory over Purdue and had some asking if they could score enough to keep up with a fairly potent Illinois offense.

"Yeah, I think we answered that pretty well," Cook said. "I think the whole offense was clicking — the pass game, the receivers were catching it downfield, getting yards after the catch, the running backs were running hard, the offensive line was blocking well in the pass game and run game. We were able to get in a groove early and things just kept clicking."

It did take a little time for things to click — on both sides of the ball.

Illinois went 53 yards on 12 plays to open the game and took a 3-0 lead on a 31-yard field goal by Taylor Zalewski. However, it wasn't long before the Michigan State defense started imposing its will.

Early in the second quarter, it produced the big play that sparked the entire team when Shilique Calhoun forced a fumble on an ill-fated reverse and the ball

Freshman running back Delton Williams celebrates a big play.

Michigan State 42, Illinois 3

Mark Scarpinato(right) and Trae Waynes (15) keep Martize Barr(7) away from the ball.

was recovered by Marcus Rush. Four plays later, Langford scored on a 1-yard run to put the Spartans ahead, 7-3.

The Illini came right back, getting all the way to the Michigan State 1-yard line, but were stuffed on two straight plays, turning the ball back over to the Spartans.

"It was huge because we kept points off the board because of the fact it was fourth down," said linebacker Max Bullough, who teamed up with Darqueze Dennard to stop running back Jon Davis on the fourth-down play. "We really hadn't been able to build momentum on offense or defense up until that point and it was a springboard for the rest of the game."

With 99 yards of the field staring them in the face, the offense proceeded to put together one of its best drives of the season, going the length of the field in 8:08 and finishing with a 29-yard touchdown pass from Cook to Bennie Fowler.

While the drive itself was impressive, the

end was bizarre.

Michigan State had moved to the Illinois 15 and faced a first down, but two straight sacks left them at the 29-yard line, the clock ticking down on the half. Cook then scrambled to his left on third down and fired a pass near the goal line and into double coverage.

Illinois defensive back Jaylen Dunlap got his hands on the ball, but it bounced in the air and Fowler grabbed it as he fell back into the end zone for a touchdown, giving Michigan State the 14-3 lead with nine seconds to play in the half.

"That was me just counting on Bennie and Bennie being capable of making a play like that," Cook said. "If I just put it out there, he can make something out of it. It was me having faith in him and he made an amazing play."

Michigan State kept on rolling in the third quarter, going 75 yards on 10 plays on the half's opening drive to take a 21-3 lead. Lang-

Michigan State 42, Illinois 3

ford did the bulk of the work on the ground before Cook capped the drive with a 13-yard touchdown pass to tight end Josiah Price.

Langford added a 7-yard touchdown run late in the third quarter to make it 28-3, and the Spartans opened the fourth quarter with a 47-yard touchdown pass from Cook to Keith Mumphery to extend their lead to 35-3. Freshman Delton Williams tacked on the final points when he scored on a 42-yard run midway through the fourth quarter. He gained 78 yards on just five carries while Nick Hill ran 13 times for 70 yards.

It was a performance that had Illinois coach Tim Beckman searching for answers.

"I've been around college ball a long time and they have got a very, very good defense," Beckman said. "The first half, you've got to score. We can't have a penalty negate a score.

You can't not score when the ball is inside the 5-yard line. You've got to score touchdowns. We have to do that as an offensive football team. We can't let teams drive 99 yards and have stupid penalties. ... The last three teams we've played have only lost one Big Ten game. They're pretty good football teams."

And it appears now that Michigan State has proved just how good it can be, sitting alone in first place of the Big Ten's Legends Division.

"Good things are happening," Dantonio said. "We have a nice foundation. We're 7-1 and, more importantly, are 4-0 in the conference and sit on top in the Legends. We've got a strong defense, our offense is coming, we run the football and have got balance. We've got to take care of business, but we'll take it one game at a time."

MSU QB Connor Cook (18) and Trevon Pendleton (37) have plenty to celebrate after their win.

A-MAIZED AND BLUE!

Michigan State 29, Michigan 6

Michigan State dismantles Michigan, erases any doubts about defense

Saturday, November 2, 2013 | East Lansing

Story by Matt Charboneau | Photos by Dale G. Young and John T. Greilick

East Lansing — Early in the week, Michigan State linebacker Max Bullough was asked if the Spartans' defense would be up to the challenge against one of the better offenses in the nation when it faced Michigan on Saturday.

The senior captain didn't especially appreciate the question, rattling off all the offenses the Spartans had shut down already this season. He mentioned Brian Kelly and Notre Dame, the power running game at Iowa and the high-powered attack at Illinois.

Michigan State handled them all — dominated, Bullough said.

After four quarters at Spartan Stadium on Saturday, there can be no further doubt about Michigan State's defense.

In one of its most dominating perfor-

Max Bullough (40) brings down Michigan running back Fitz Toussaint.

Michigan State 29, Michigan 6

mance of the past three seasons, No. 24 Michigan State held No. 23 Michigan to 168 total yards and minus-48 yards rushing while piling up seven sacks and 11 tackles-for-loss in a 29-6 victory in front of 76,306 at Spartan Stadium on Saturday.

"It was a great football day for Michigan State," coach Mark Dantonio said. "Defensively, we've just been dominant. (Opponents) haven't scored a touchdown in the last three weeks, so we really have been dominant. In modern football, you just don't see that very often, and that's a credit to our staff."

The last touchdown allowed by Michigan State came against Indiana on Oct. 12 and on Saturday, the Spartans held the Wolverines to their lowest rushing total ever. It showed this game was far more one-sided than the

Sparty breaks out a new look in the spirit of the Paul Bunyan Trophy.

one two years ago — a 28-14 Michigan State victory — that Michigan offensive tackle Taylor Lewan referenced early in the week when he said his team was "bullied" the last time it visited East Lansing.

"Two years ago was nothing," said Michigan State linebacker Denicos Allen, who had

Michigan State 29, Michigan 6

Shilique Calhoun (89) brings down Michigan QB Devin Gardner.

two sacks and led the team with nine tackles. "It was a lot worse today, and I think they felt it."

Lewan couldn't argue.

"Yeah, I think that's exactly what it was," he said. "I think a lot of this game absolutely falls on this offensive line. They ran a bunch of group blitzes, a lot of the same blitzes they ran in 2011. ... when it came down to it, we couldn't pick it up. That's our job."

While many of the negative rushing yards were because of the sacks and a bad snap that went 20 yards in the wrong direction for Michigan, the domination was hard to ignore. Running back Fitz Toussaint gained 20 yards on eight carries and quarterback Devin

Michigan State 29, Michigan 6

Gardner was knocked out of the game for Michigan's final drive.

"We're going to bully people — that's the game of football," Michigan State defensive coordinator Pat Narduzzi said. "We didn't want any personal fouls — we had one stupid one, I think on special teams at the end — we talked really about not getting any penalties. ... They've got a good football team, but we've got a great football team."

And it's a football team that has won five of the last six meetings in the rivalry and improves to 8-1 overall and 5-0 in the Big Ten, putting a stranglehold on first place in the Legends Division with three games to play.

The Spartans have a bye next week before heading to Nebraska to play a team one game behind in the division at a stadium Michigan State has never won.

"We are just ready to take it week by week," Bullough said. "We have a bye week, and then Taylor Martinez, who has torched us the last couple years. We haven't been able to beat Nebraska. So we have another challenge ahead of us."

Ed Davis (43) brings down Michigan QB Devin Gardner.

Michigan State 29, Michigan 6

Ed Davis (43) and Denicos Allen celebrate a big tackle.

No. 23 Michigan (6-2, 2-2) came into the game averaging better than 445 yards a game but never got much going against the No. 1-ranked defense in the nation.

And when Michigan State quarterback Connor Cook scored on a 1-yard touchdown run with 10:31 to play in the game, it all but sealed the Wolverines' fate, one that was assured when Jeremy Langford scored on a 40-yard run with just less than three minutes to play.

"Lot of negative-yardage plays," Michigan coach Brady Hoke said. "There were some pretty good runs once in a while in there, but when you snap the ball for a 20-yard loss and you get sacked I don't know how many times, so your yardage part of it isn't very good.

"You put yourself behind the eight ball a little bit not executing, and then you're forced into doing some things you don't want to do the whole time. It's not just the (offensive) line, there's backs involved, there's routes involved, there's timing. All of those issues are a part of it."

The biggest issue was the beating Gardner took. He was sacked seven times and knocked to the ground countless times as Michigan State's Shilique Calhoun and Ed Davis recorded 2.5 sacks each.

"Yeah, it feels good, anytime you can press the quarterback like we did," Bullough said. "You talk about

Michigan State 29, Michigan 6

James Kittredge (99) and teammates hoist the Paul Bunyan Trophy.

how it was a physical beatdown out here. I think anyone watching or in the game would agree with you. Yeah, that is a complete game for us."

It was so complete that Michigan's best moments were limited to early in the game.

Gardner connected with Jeremy Gallon for a 35-yard gain on the first play from scrimmage, and Gardner hit Gallon two more times on the opening drive, each time for 11 yards, as the Wolverines got inside the Spartans 25. But a sack of Gardner by Allen and Calhoun on second down pushed the Wolver-

ines back, and they settled for a 49-yard field goal from Matt Wile to take a 3-0 lead with 10:38 to play in the first quarter.

After Michigan State answered with a 40-yard field goal from Michael Geiger, the teams traded field goals again in the second quarter before the Michigan State offense started to find a rhythm and put together its best drive of the game, going 75 yards on 10 plays, taking a 13-6 lead into halftime on a 14-yard pass from Cook to Bennie Fowler.

Michigan State kept its offensive momentum going to open the second half, putting to-

Michigan State 29, Michigan 6

Mark Dantonio shares a pregame moment with his wife, Becky.

gether a 10-play, 46-yard drive that ended with Geiger's third field goal of the game, a 35-yarder that extended the Spartans' lead to 16-6 with just less than 10 minutes left in the third quarter.

Gardner finished 14-for-27 for 210 yards, but a late interception by Michigan State's Darqueze Dennard ended any shot at a comeback.

Langford finished with 26 carries for 120 yards for the Spartans, the fourth straight week he has gone over the 100-yard mark, while Fowler caught six passes for 75 yards and Tony Lippett had five grabs for 62 yards.

Michigan State 29, Michigan 6

Balance of instate rivalry shifts MSU's way in punishing victory

By Bob Wojnowski

East Lansing — Michigan State kept pounding forward and Michigan kept going backward, and that's where the rivalry sits right now, only one tough guy on this block. You can't say this was an eye-opener because we've seen it before, although not this punishing.

The Spartans splattered the Wolverines, 29-6, Saturday and if that counts as bullying, they might as well keep it up until someone stops them. Afterward, Brady Hoke didn't say much and Mark Dantonio didn't need to say anything. The numbers said it all.

The Wolverines were embarrassed, overwhelmed at times, and Devin Gardner had no chance. The Spartans sacked him seven times, and when you add up all the negative plays, the Wolverines finished with an astounding minus-48 yards rushing.

Is Michigan State's defense that stiflingly good, or is Michigan's blocking that bad? The answer: Yes. The Wolverines vowed not to

Jeremy Langford's touchdown sends the Spartan Stadium crowd into a frenzy.

Michigan State 29, Michigan 6

Jeremy Langford feels the heat of Frank Clark and Michigan's defensive line.

get shoved around again — offensive tackle Taylor Lewan had brought up the bully angle — and then went out and got shoved around even more.

"I think we did it worse today," Michigan State linebacker Denicos Allen said. "Two years ago was nothing. It was a lot worse, and I think they felt it. ... Call us what you want, call us little brother, big brother. But when it's on the field, we show who's the big brother and who's the little brother."

That's hitting where it hurts, and the Wolverines felt it. Gardner couldn't even finish the game because, according to Hoke, he was "beat up." It essentially was over moments after it looked like it was about to get interesting. Raymon Taylor intercepted a Connor Cook pass and Michigan had the ball at

Michigan State 29, Michigan 6

Michigan State's 41 late in the third quarter, trailing 16-6.

Then Gardner was dropped for a 5-yard loss, sacked by Allen for a 9-yard loss and sacked by Allen and Ed Davis for a 7-yard loss. Just like that, it was fourth-and-31, which actually looked manageable compared to the fourth-and-48 the Wolverines faced earlier in the game.

Al Borges' game plan was oddly scattered and he needs to reevaluate what he's doing, especially with that young and woe-ful offensive line. But frankly, Pat Narduzzi's blitz-happy defense would have shattered it regardless. Michigan State's defense is No. 1 in the nation, and people can pick apart the lack of quality competition all they want. But this group is loaded, breathtaking to watch, even for the Spartans' offensive guys.

"I just watch on the Jumbotron, and pretty much the only thing I saw was them in the backfield the whole game," Cook said. "It was almost like Devin couldn't even breathe."

The pattern is growing, and impossible to

Connor Cook (18) and Bennie Fowler (13) let the celebration start at Spartan Stadium.

Michigan State 29, Michigan 6

explain away. With five victories in the past six meetings, Michigan State is the type of grinding, rumbling team Michigan is trying to become. Hoke has a bigger issue than he probably expected, and deep into his third season, the Wolverines look no tougher in the trenches.

Since Dantonio took over in 2007, the Wolverines' point total in this game has dropped every year, from 28 to 21 to 20 to 17 to 14 to 12 to six, and they haven't scored a touchdown the past two meetings. Dantonio knows the rivalry, relishes the rivalry and finds players who want to line up and slug it out. Michigan won 12-10 last season, a brief respite. You can't control your own state if you can't control your own lines, and Michigan State is in control right now.

"We're not trying to go out and bully anybody," Dantonio said, his postgame mood respectfully reserved. "They got big guys too. But we're gonna play hard, we're gonna play like I've been taught throughout my coaching career. We're gonna play good defense, we're gonna try to run the ball and we're gonna try to physically win."

That's what they did, all day long, up and down the wet field on a drizzly day. The Spartans have so many defensive stars, it's hard to pick one, although Allen, Shilique Calhoun (2.5 more sacks) and Max Bullough are great places to start.

Now the Spartans can aim even higher, in command of the Legends Division at 8-1 (5-0 Big Ten). With their remaining schedule — bye, at Nebraska, at Northwestern, home to Minnesota — they're a heavy favorite to reach the championship game, where they'd likely face Ohio State.

This was one of Dantonio's finest mo-

ments, and as the final seconds ticked away, he pointed toward the celebrating student section, and the roar grew. You'd think by now, with Michigan's struggles, everyone would be done with the big brother-little brother talk. Clearly, it has motivated the Spartans since Mike Hart stirred it back in 2007, and they're not letting it go until someone takes it from them.

If Michigan wants a return to old brotherhoods, it has to figure some things out, and it isn't as simple as better play-calling from Borges and Greg Mattison. As awful as the offense looked, especially after a bye, there weren't many answers to Michigan State's defensive ferocity.

The interior of Michigan's offensive line is young, but it shouldn't be that weak. Fitz Toussaint had nowhere to run and wasn't effective blocking. If you can't run the ball and get sacked every other time you drop back, the options dwindle.

Hoke looked a bit shell-shocked afterward, and defended Borges' game plan. That's what a program leader is supposed to do, maintain calm even though repair work is obvious. I asked Hoke if the recent streak indicated a widening gap between the programs.

"I don't think there is a gap," he said. "I think they played awfully well, executed awfully well, and I don't think we did."

Whatever it is — a gap, a blip, a resounding shift — it's still there. It was thoroughly evident on this day, in Gardner's pained expression and in the numbing numbers. And especially in the Spartans' grim-faced determination, as if they knew exactly what they could do, and the Wolverines had no idea what was coming.

SPARTANS
CONQUER
NEBRASKA

Michigan State 41, Nebraska 28

Michigan State up to its old tricks in win, controls Legends destiny

Saturday, November 16, 2013 | Lincoln, Nebraska
Story by Matt Charboneau | Photos by Dale G. Young

Lincoln, Neb. — Late Saturday evening, with the sun setting on Memorial Stadium and the full moon rising, Charles Schulz would have been proud.

Why exactly would the creator of "Peanuts" care about No. 14 Michigan State's matchup with Nebraska in a game that would go a long way in determining which team wins the Legends Division and plays in the Big Ten championship game?

Because with the game still in the balance, Michigan State coach Mark Dantonio — quickly becoming the master at trickery — made the call that would help the Spartans cap off a fourth-quarter drive and put the game away, earning a 41-28 victory in front of 90,872.

It was fourth-and-1 at the Nebraska 27, less than 10 minutes to play and Michigan State holding a slim six-point lead.

That's when Dantonio called it — "Charlie Brown."

Instead of kicker Michael Geiger attempting a 45-yard field goal, he swung his leg at a ball that wasn't there, just like the lead character in the famous comic strip. Instead, punter and holder Mike Sadler was running into the middle of the line, grinding away for 3 yards and a

Kurtis Drummond celebrates after a big play for the Spartans.

Michigan State 41, Nebraska 28

Damon Knox (93) reacts after bringing down a Nebraska ballcarrier.

first down. Four plays later, the Spartans were in the end zone thanks to a third-down strike from Connor Cook to Keith Mumphery.

"Well at some point in time, your head football coach has to take some chances," Dantonio explained, a big smile on his face and green Gatorade in hand. "I told our football team at halftime, 'Hey, we are going to roll the dice.' I already made up my mind on that series, if we got within field-goal range we were running the field goal fake, 'Charlie Brown.' So that is what we decided to do,

Michigan State 41, Nebraska 28

Keith Mumphery (25) is mobbed by teammates after a huge touchdown.

then when we got up there and it was fourth-and-1, and I thought maybe we should just go for it but it was too late, it worked."

It sure did, and not only was it the first time Michigan State has defeated Nebraska, it puts the Spartans (9-1, 6-0 Big Ten) in control of the Legends Division with just two games to play. At least a share of the title is clinched, but this team is playing for a trip to Indianapolis and the Big Ten championship game. One win in the final two weeks or a Minnesota loss will sew up that, as well.

Michigan State 41, Nebraska 28

But to get to that point, Michigan State had to take care of business at a stadium in which it had never won. In fact, it was a stadium where they had never really played well, a 24-3 loss in 2011 still fresh on the minds of many.

However, in addition to the trickery, the Spartans were the beneficiary of five Nebraska turnovers on a day its defense gave up 392 yards, the most it has all season.

"If you go in our locker room right now, there's a lot of happy guys," linebacker Max Bullough said. "There's a lot of guys that are happy that we won, but there's some guys that are not necessarily pumped about our perfor-

mance on defense. We're not going to ignore the elephant in the room. We didn't play as well as we wanted to. (But) we'd rather be sitting here talking about what we can fix while we're in the winning column."

The Cornhuskers (7-3, 4-2) did their best to oblige as the Spartans scored 24 points off turnovers.

"You had an opportunity to take away five turnovers," Dantonio said. "It is tough to lose a football game when that happens."

It started on the third play from scrimmage when Nebraska running back Terrell Newby couldn't hang on to a pitch and Shilique Calhoun was there to scoop up the loose

Coach Mark Dantonio has his hands full against Nebraska.

Michigan State 41, Nebraska 28

ball. Michigan State turned that into a 45-yard field goal from Geiger and an early 3-0 lead.

The Huskers followed with two more first-quarter turnovers, the second coming when Jordan Westerkamp fumbled a punt and the Spartans took over at the Nebraska 8. Two plays later, freshman R.J. Shelton ran the ball in from 5 yards out to give Michigan State a 10-0 lead.

Nebraska bounced back with a five-play drive that lasted just 2:13 and cut the Michigan State lead to 10-7 late in the first quarter. Quarterback Tommy Armstrong Jr. connected with Sam Burtch on a 32-yard touchdown pass when Michigan State blew the coverage, leaving Burtch all alone to walk into the end zone.

The Spartans extended their lead to 13-7 on a 26-yard field goal from Geiger with 10:29 to play in the second quarter and later capitalized again when Armstrong fumbled on third down deep in his own end and the ball was recovered by Isaiah Lewis. Three plays later, Jeremy Langford scored on a 6-yard run to give the Spartans a 20-7 halftime lead.

The Huskers struck quickly in the second half, going 63 yards in just 1:01 to cut the Michigan State lead to 20-14 on a 51-yard run by Imani Cross. But another turnover by Armstrong, this time a fumble near his own goal line, allowed Michigan State to add to its lead. Trae Waynes covered the ball at the 3. On the next play, Langford scored his second touchdown to put the Spartans up 27-14 with 5:26 to play in the third quarter.

"We just made too many mistakes to overcome," Nebraska coach Bo Pelini said. "It's hard to be minus-five in the turnover category and win a football game against a quality football team."

The Huskers kept hope alive late in the third quarter when Armstrong found Kenny Bell on a 38-yard touchdown pass, but the Spartans responded with a 75-yard, 10-play drive, kept alive by the fake field goal.

Langford added a 37-yard touchdown run late to cap the Michigan State scoring while Ameer Abdullah caught a 12-yard scoring pass with 10 seconds to play for the Huskers. Langford finished with a career-high 151 yards on 32 carries and three touchdowns while Cook was 15-for-31 for 193 yards.

Nebraska ran for 182 yards, the first team all season to surpass 100 yards against Michigan State, while Abdullah finished with 123 yards on 22 carries.

"We've run the football on them for three years," Pelini said. "We beat this football team the past two years. They're a quality football team. But we've run the football on them before, and we'll run it on them again."

What the Huskers won't be doing is playing for a Big Ten title. Michigan State, on the other hand, looks like it will and gets a chance to assure that next week at Northwestern. It's a far cry from the last Michigan State team that played at Nebraska, or last year's group that barely reached a bowl game.

"We can sit here and talk about how they gashed us in the run game or how they had a few plays, but we won," Bullough said. "That's the difference between being 7-6 or whatever it is and hopefully competing for the championship at the end of the year. I think that's something that you earn in the offseason and it's something that you earn each week. That's something that you can't put a name on, you can't put a price on."

MICHIGAN STATE **30** NORTHWESTERN **6**

HATS OFF
TO THEM

Michigan State 30, Northwestern 6

Spartans thump Northwestern, earn trip to Big Ten championship game

Saturday, November 23, 2013 | Evanston, Ill.
Story by Matt Charboneau | Photos by Dale G. Young

Evanston, Ill. – Winning the Legends Division title in the Big Ten comes complete with a nice, shiny new trophy.

It's like the one Michigan State won two years ago, and on Saturday at Ryan Field, the 13th-ranked Spartans secured another with a 30-6 victory over Northwestern in front of a pro-Michigan State crowd of 40,013 on a chilly day.

But coach Mark Dantonio wasn't looking

Redshirt freshman tight end Josiah Price celebrates a 15-yard touchdown catch.

Michigan State 30, Northwestern 6

MSU's defense swarmed Northwestern ballcarriers all day.

for a picture with the new hardware. Nope, he wanted something everyone could have a piece of — a hat.

"That was more important for me," Dantonio said. "It's all symbolic of the same thing, but I said all week long, 'Let's put a hat on.'"

The Spartans (10-1, 7-0 Big Ten) did just that, clinching a spot in the Big Ten championship game for the second time in three seasons. They will face No. 3 Ohio State, which secured the Leaders Division title on Saturday

with a victory over Indiana.

"It feels good," senior cornerback Darqueze Dennard said. "There is a lot of hard work that we put in through the offseason and all the work we put in this season. Winning this game and knowing we're going to Indianapolis is a great feeling. We knew (in August) what type of team we had. ... It's a great feeling right now, seeing it all come together."

The feeling took about a quarter to show

Michigan State 30, Northwestern 6

Connor Cook rallied his team for a big road victory over Northwestern.

up Saturday, but when it did, there seemed to be little Northwestern could do to stop it.

Michigan State dominated for the most part and rolled up 464 yards of total offense and limited the Wildcats to just 95 in the second half while intercepting three passes.

It was another outstanding day for running back Jeremy Langford, who carried 25 times for 150 yards and two touchdowns while going over the 1,000-yard mark for the season. Quarterback Connor Cook also was impressive, going 16-for-24 for a career-high 293 yards and two touchdowns.

And when it was over and the players had their hats, the celebration began in the locker room — players and coaches dancing — much like the scene publicized after last week's win over Nebraska. This time it was offensive coordinator Dave Warner who danced for the team.

"Dave Warner pulled a Mark Staten and made a complete fool of himself," offensive lineman Dan France said. "It was pretty impressive for an old guy. Then Travis (Jackson) came in and ended it with his little dance."

There's no doubt these are fun times for the Spartans, who are 7-0 in Big Ten play for just the third time with a chance for their first-ever 8-0 mark next week. But that's what happens when you go from a team with one of the most inept offenses in the conference the first four weeks of the season to one of the most potent.

"I'm so proud of the guys for all the criticism we took early in the year," Cook said. "We put our heads down and worked hard and didn't listen to the criticism or harsh words from what the media was saying, what the fans were saying, and kept working. I'm real proud of them."

It has created a team that just a few weeks ago was relying on its top-rated defense to

Michigan State 30, Northwestern 6

Jeremy Langford(33) breaks free for a touchdown and leaves Wildcat Ibraheim Campbell(24) on his face.

win games to one that is balanced, winning by scoring points and stuffing opponents. The defense was solid again Saturday, limiting Northwestern to 80 yards on the ground, but it was the big plays on offense that were key.

After Northwestern (4-7, 0-7) opened the scoring with a 22-yard field goal from Jeff Budzien, Michigan State started rolling. Langford capped an 11-play drive with a 20-yard touchdown run to put the Spartans ahead 7-3 with 8:22 left in the second quarter.

Late in the second quarter, Michigan State got its first big play to extend its lead when Bennie Fowler scored on an 87-yard touchdown pass to put the Spartans up 14-3 with 4:31 left in the first half. The Spartans were

facing a third-and-5 deep in their own end when Cook lofted a pass down the sideline to Fowler. Northwestern cornerback Matthew Harris barely got a hand on the ball, but Fowler came up with it and went untouched the rest of the way to the end zone.

"We wanted to get the first down for sure and with Bennie, if I just put it out there he would have a chance," Cook said of the play. "So I checked to a go route and he made a great play. I think the defender, if he was facing me, could have picked it off. That was just me counting on (Fowler)."

Northwestern managed a late field goal to cut the halftime lead to 14-6, but its options basically ran out at that point as Michigan

Michigan State 30, Northwestern 6

State allowed just 95 total yards in the second half and got two interceptions from Kurtis Drummond and another from Darqueze Dennard.

The Spartans scored on the opening drive of the half as Michael Geiger booted a 37-yard field goal to extend the lead to 17-6 with 11:33 left in the third quarter. It added another score later in the third quarter with an eight-play, 87-yard drove that ended with a 15-yard touchdown pass from Cook to Josiah Price with five minutes left in the third quarter. The extra point was blocked, leaving Michigan State ahead 23-6.

The Spartans capped the scoring after Drummond's interception set them up at the Wildcats' 37. On the next play, Langford scored his second touchdown of the game to put the Spartans up 30-6 with 12:37 to play.

It was another tough day for the home team, which hasn't won since late September.

"It's definitely been a rough experience," defensive lineman Tyler Scott said. "You never want to lose a game, but to lose seven in a row, it's challenging. The thing about our team, though, we've persevered and we've fought every game. We've been in a lot of them. Today wasn't that same way, but we've persevered and our attitudes haven't changed."

And it hasn't changed for Michigan State, which now faces Minnesota at home next week before heading to Indianapolis to play for the Big Ten title against the Buckeyes.

"I love the hat," said Langford, who went over the 100-yard mark for the sixth straight game, "but hopefully we can switch it out in a couple of weeks."

MSU fans know whom the biggest Big Ten showdown of the year will be against.

MICHIGAN STATE **14** MINNESOTA **3**

EIGHT AND-OH!

Michigan State 14, Minnesota 3

Michigan State stifles Minnesota for perfect Big Ten record

Saturday, November 30, 2013 | East Lansing
Story by Matt Charboneau | Photos by Dale G. Young

East Lansing — While Saturday's victory over Minnesota was far from a masterpiece, what it represented was pretty darned impressive.

No. 11 Michigan State got 134 yards rushing from Jeremy Langford and its defense forced three turnovers in a 14-3 victory over Minnesota at Spartan Stadium in the regular-season finale.

In the process, the Spartans capped off the first 8-0 Big Ten mark in school history while going 7-0 at home and winning 11 games for the third time in four seasons.

"I'm very proud of our football team," coach Mark Dantonio said. "Forty wins in four years, 11 wins this

Tony Lippett (14) came up big for MSU as it secured an undefeated record in Big Ten play.

Mark Scarpinato (97) has reason to strut after MSU stopped the Gophers on three straight plays at the one-yard line in the second quarter.

Michigan State 14, Minnesota 3

year. You're going to have some games where you've got to reach back and scratch and dig for things and we were able to do that today. I'm very proud of our guys, our senior leaders. I've said all along that we win because of our chemistry. I believe that, I believe that totally.

"(We're) 7-0 at home for the third time in four years, 8-0 in the conference for the first time that's ever been done, 11-1 for the third time in three years. Not too many football programs in the country can say those things, so I just want to congratulate our football team and what they've been able to accomplish."

The Spartans (11-1, 8-0 Big Ten) got a 15-yard touchdown run from Langford on their opening drive of the game and a 12-yard

Denzel Drone (42) led a pack of Spartans on this tackle.

Michigan State 14, Minnesota 3

Senior Day brings out the emotions of those playing in their last game at Spartan Stadium, including Danny Folino (19), Kyler Ellsworth (41) and Denzel Drone (42).

scoring pass from Connor Cook to Josiah Price on the first drive of the second half to provide all the scoring it needed.

Now the Spartans head to the Big Ten Championship game next week for a meeting with Ohio State, which capped off its perfect season by hanging on to beat Michigan.

"I'm really excited," defensive coordinator Pat Narduzzi said. "I got excited after the game last week. We talked about being 4-0 in November and taking it one at a time. Championships are won in November and we have an opportunity to clean up something from a year ago.

"So, we'll be live on defense again this week, I guarantee it. That was a mistake from a year ago. It'll be all out."

The mistake Narduzzi talked about was not going live headed into the Ohio State game last season. The Spartans paid the price as Buckeyes quarterback Braxton Miller ran for 136 yards and threw a 63-yard touchdown pass to Devin Smith in the third quarter to spark a 17-16 victory for Ohio State.

"That's what we need to do and that's what we're going to do," linebacker Max Bullough said. "That was a mistake that we made previously. When you've got a good quarterback, a guy that can run and pass like Braxton Miller, you need to be prepared. You need to be able

Michigan State 14, Minnesota 3

to take him down to the ground. Even today I thought we missed some tackles on that tailback who's a good player."

That tailback was Minnesota's David Cobb, who became just the second back this season to go over 100 yards against the Spartans, gaining 101 on 27 carries.

"Michigan State is the No. 1 defense in the country, period, and when you're No. 1 in the country in defense you've got a chance to win a lot of games," Minnesota coach Jerry Kill said. "I can't say enough good things about what they do, and I've got a great deal of respect for the program and again, I think we gave a great effort and came up short and we feel bad about that, but we need to heal up and we know we're still playing, so that's a great advantage for us. It gives us an opportunity to still have a lot to accomplish this season."

While the Gophers (8-4, 4-4) got their share of yards, they were unable to get in the end zone. The only points they did manage came on a 21-yard field goal by Chris Hawthorne in the second quarter.

Minnesota had a shot late to cut into Michigan State's lead, but a sack and fumble by Gophers quarterback Mitch Leidner ended the threat. Shilique Calhoun and Tyler Hoover combined on the sack and Hoover came up with the ball.

"They can drive down the field as many times as they want, but that's not going to win the game," Bullough said. "It might change field position and time of possession, but if we just don't let them in the end zone. At the end of the day they can have as many yards as they want, we can be mad about that, they had 180 rush yards or whatever it was (124), but they had three points. They had three points, let's think about that. It's a Big Ten team that's won a lot of games and they had three points. In the end that's what matters and that's what wins football games."

And the Spartans have won enough to put themselves in the spot they hoped for before the season began — a shot at the Rose Bowl.

"That's a goal that we have not yet accomplished," Dantonio said. "So that's the No. 1 goal — to be the outright Big Ten champion. The way the format is structured now would be something that would be very important to this program. Obviously to get to the Rose Bowl is something that we've aspired to since the day we set foot on this campus back in 1995. When we came back in 2007, the same thing was talked about on the day that I got the job.

"So obviously it's always been in the background, pushing us forward and propelling us and giving us added enthusiasm for what we do."

MSU athletic director Mark Hollis, left, congratulates Bennie Fowler during Senior Day.

Michigan State 14, Minnesota 3

Potentially BCS-bound for first time, MSU acts like it's been here before

By John Niyo

East Lansing — Been there, haven't done that.

As a coach, that's the ideal scenario, motivationally speaking. And for Michigan State's Mark Dantonio, that's probably what made the relatively subdued postgame atmosphere here Saturday so strangely satisfying.

The Spartans sent their seniors out in style, with a 14-3 win over Minnesota that capped another unbeaten home schedule and the school's first perfect Big Ten regular season since 1966.

But even that uncharted territory felt like old news by the time the head coach and his players met with the media afterward. And that bodes well for the immediate future, as Michigan State (11-1) prepares to face Ohio State (12-0) for the outright Big Ten champi-

Darien Harris (45), Trae Waynes (15) and the Spartans had plenty to celebrate.

Michigan State 14, Minnesota 3

Mark Scarpinato (97) and Denicos Allen (28) helped shut down the Gophers.

Michigan State 14, Minnesota 3

onship next weekend in Indianapolis.

"We've been here before," Dantonio said. "We've won 11 games before. And it feels good. You feel like you've attained a goal. But at the same time, nobody's giving anybody Gatorade showers. We have one more to go."

That's the one that really counts. That's the one that can set this team apart from all the others. And for the Spartans, who'd already booked their trip to Indianapolis with last

week's win at Northwestern, that's the one they finally can talk about now.

"It's a lot that I've got building up," senior linebacker Denicos Allen said. "And I can't wait to let it all out."

Well, the wait is nearly over: Bring on the Buckeyes.

"My kids said, 'Dad, you want us to DVR the Ohio State game?'" defensive coordinator Pat Narduzzi joked late Saturday afternoon,

The Spartan defense prevented a single touchdown against the Minnesota offense.

Michigan State 14, Minnesota 3

only moments before Ohio State managed to escape with a win in Ann Arbor. "And I said, 'Please.'"

And thanks again to his defense, the Spartans are headed to Indianapolis on a positive note.

BCS-bound?

Michigan State's offense sputtered Saturday in ways it hadn't in weeks, failing to convert a third down all afternoon (0-for-8) and finishing with just 51 offensive snaps. And while the defense had some issues of its own — Minnesota's David Cobb rushed for 101 yards, and the Gophers held a 2-to-1 advantage in possession time — the final outcome never really was in doubt.

"They had three points," senior linebacker Max Bullough said. "Let's think about that: That's a Big Ten team that has won a lot of games, and they had three points. In the end, that's what matters."

What matters now, of course, is beating Ohio State for an automatic berth to the Rose Bowl, though the consolation prize might still be — should be? — a BCS at-large berth. Maybe even a trip to Pasadena, after the way the rest of Saturday's chaos unfolded.

Dantonio wasn't shy about lobbying for one when asked to do so Saturday — "Two teams from the Big Ten should go," he said — but all his talk about the "risk" involved in playing in a conference championship game may prove unnecessary in the wake of Wisconsin's stunning loss to Penn State on Saturday.

"Hopefully we're attractive enough, if we lose," Dantonio said. "But we don't plan on losing."

Like I said, they've been there and done that. And they certainly don't plan on doing it again, with the memory of that 42-39 loss to Wisconsin in the inaugural Big Ten title game two years ago still lingering for many.

"We lost the game on one of the last plays of the game, so there's not too much I would change," Dantonio said, before adding with a

laugh, "Other than the last play of the game, or something like that."

That, of course, is a reference to Michigan State's punt-block attempt with under 2 minutes left in the 2011 title game, a play that drew a controversial flag — negating Keshawn Martin's potential game-winning return — and effectively ended the Spartans' chances.

Safety Isaiah Lewis, the player who got flagged, said, "You don't even understand, the last time I was in Indianapolis, for me, I was heartbroken."

We might not understand, but his teammates do.

Eyes on the prize

The strength of this team is in its senior leadership, particularly on defense. And the look in Bullough's eyes as he talked about the defense going live in practice this week tells you everything you need to know about the Spartans' motivation. If any team can shut down Ohio State's Braxton Miller and Carlos Hyde, it's probably this one, and they know it. But just in case, they're going to prove it with pads on against the scout team led by freshman Damion Terry. ("He needs to rest up this weekend," said cornerback Darqueze Dennard, "because he's gonna have a long week.") And then they'll head to Indianapolis with something to prove.

Underdogs?

Yep, maybe by a touchdown or more.

Overlooked?

"Let's hope so," Dantonio said, grinning.

But overwhelmed? No chance.

"Just knowing we got so close," Dennard said. "Everybody who was down there knows. Walking off the field without them roses in our mouths, it left a bad taste."

Asked what his message will be to some of the Michigan State underclassmen this week, he replied, flatly, "You don't want to have that feeling that I had."

No, what they want is what they've got now. And Saturday, it felt pretty good.

Head Coach Mark Dantonio

Dantonio's intense drive brings success to Spartans

Coach is comfortable in his skin, surroundings at MSU

By Lynn Henning

Coach Mark Dantonio lets an official know his side of the story.

Head Coach Mark Dantonio

East Lansing — It's the 21st day of November, the 11th week of a typically nerves-shredding college football season, and Mark Dantonio doesn't show it.

He sits in his second-floor office at the Skandalaris Center, a long par-3 from Spartan Stadium, and the man's pulse is too low, the look is too casual, the voice is too measured for a coach whose team is playing for the Big Ten football championship.

But isn't this all a reflection of everything Dantonio has crafted? That he set in motion seven years ago this week when he arrived

from Cincinnati? Isn't the 11-1 record, the gray sweat pants and dark green, long-sleeve Nike shirt he features as he sits in an occasional chair, the utter comfort of an office as neatly furnished as the man's life — isn't this the simple product of what Michigan State's best football architect since the Biggie Munn-Duffy Daugherty era has put into place?

Of course it is. It is why his boss, Mark Hollis, the athletic director who headed the safari that returned him to East Lansing, helped hire him in 2006.

Steady recruiting heavy on projections

Coach Mark Dantonio patrols the sideline early this season.

Head Coach Mark Dantonio

and light on star-ratings has been the concrete and brickwork for one of America's best defenses. Low attrition, healthy graduation rates, red-shirting good athletes in a bid to help them help the team and themselves flourish during a five-year stay in East Lansing, and finally, knowing how to make that personnel function at something close to optimum levels — this is why Dantonio can look in late November as if he's sitting down for a game of cards rather than bracing for Ohio State and a rare shot at a Rose Bowl trip.

Confidence in who you and your team are, the necessity of preparation and the dimin-ishing returns from over-fixations, these are the fine lines the 57-year-old coach and his staff have been able to etch as one of the Big Ten's best recent examples of pure football program-building evolves in East Lansing.

"We're still working 80-some-hour weeks, but if you can't get it done in 15 hours, you're not going to get it done in 17," Dantonio says, explaining the coaching staff's schedule.

Sunday, Monday, and Tuesday nights are the heavy sessions for the coach and his assistants: They begin their film reviews and meetings at some point around dawn and labor until 9:30-9:45 p.m., at which time the men

Athletic Director Mark Hollis, right, helped bring Coach Mark Dantonio to MSU in 2006.

Head Coach Mark Dantonio

head home for at least a half-decent night of spousal conversation and sleep.

Wednesday and Thursdays are what the coaching profession comes closest to terming "off-nights." They wrap up practice and can, in most cases, enjoy dinner and something approaching an evening at home. Comparatively speaking, it's domestic bliss.

"We have a schedule," Dantonio explains of his staff's autumn lifestyle. "The trick is to not waste a lot of time. You want to cover bases, but not linger.

"We watch our film. And for us, practice is where everyone has to earn his keep. But the schedule we have here is pretty much the same schedule we had at Ohio State."

That would be a reference to his time as former Ohio State coach Jim Tressel's defensive coordinator. This was before Dantonio headed to Cincinnati to make the Bearcats a relevant three-season story, after which Hollis all but told him he was returning to East Lansing, the place where from 1995-2000 he had been an assistant on the Nick Saban and Bobby Williams staffs.

"Sometimes I sit there thinking, one, two, three, four, five six, seven — wow, that's a long time," Dantonio says, speaking of his seven seasons as Spartans head coach. "At other times, it seems like I just got here.

"The number 7 in the Bible is the number for completion. But we haven't completed our mission quite yet."

Meaning: There has been no Big Ten championship since Dantonio arrived. There has been no Rose Bowl, the conventional objective for most Big Ten teams. There has been no BCS appearance.

There has been nothing close to a run for the national championship, a hoary goal conference teams other than Ohio State and

Michigan at least entertain as possible.

But the very fact Michigan State recovered from last year's madness (five losses by 13 points), and that the Spartans have shaken 11/2 seasons of Dantonio-engineered quarterback flux finally settled by Connor Cook, is affirming for Michigan State.

It returns to the rails a team and a program that had appeared to have wobbled after Dantonio's earlier breakthroughs when the Spartans won 11 games in 2010 and 2011.

But when the remainder of the team fell more into rhythm and this autumn, and the quarterback, were still moving at about the pace of a covered wagon, Dantonio pulled the trigger by pulling Andrew Maxwell. Cook has taken over and, in step with receivers rediscovering their mitts, and running back Jeremy Langford giving the ground game a jolt, Michigan State has at least found an offense that can support its defensive mashers.

As a corollary, Dantonio's offensive staffers, particularly co-coordinators Jim Bollman and Dave Warner, have been almost as loved this year as the coordinating king himself, Pat Narduzzi, who supervises the defense.

It's a program, which is what George Perles had initially installed the last time Michigan State played at Pasadena, Calif., on Jan. 1, 1988. The difference is Dantonio has shown during seven years that his program has a chance at more long-term stability than occurred under Perles, when sharing an athletic director's job, fighting with the president, and sundry distractions led to bad times and to Perles being fired in 1994.

"He's a classy guy who knows how to delegate," Perles said, speaking this week of a coach he has watched and known for almost 20 years. "He's a complete football coach and a gentleman, which is almost impossible to

Head Coach Mark Dantonio

Coach Mark Dantonio calls out to a player during the Northwestern game.

do in that, sometimes a coach has to be rough, really rough, and yet maintain a pleasing personality.

"He's simply a class guy who gets respect and the most out of his kids."

Dantonio would return the compliment in this way: He remembers last year, those crushing losses, all squeakers, one of which came courtesy of a blown call in a miserable home loss to Nebraska.

"I learned from Coach Perles," Dantonio said, "when everybody's down after a tough loss, you need to be the one who walks in and reassures everybody that it's OK. Things will

be all right. And that attitude will permeate throughout the program."

Equilibrium, in other words, is the goal. In winning. In losing. In football. In life.

Away from the Skandalaris Center, he and wife Becky are managing their marriage and parentage in happy fashion. There is a getaway home in Montague, near Muskegon, and on Lake Michigan, where the family can let down its hair and where the coach can look at something other than film. In the case of Dantonio, he enjoys fixing things, a handyman's skill he inherited from his late father, Justin, who was a crew-chief mechanic on World War II

Head Coach Mark Dantonio

bombers.

Back home, he and Becky can hit dinner at Dusty's Wine Cellars, or Noodles & Co., or wherever the spirit might take them, generally free from well-wishers who want to say thanks in the middle of Mark enjoying his sautéed perch.

"One thing about East Lansing," he says, with a nod, "they give you your space."

He had a heart attack a few minutes after the 2010 fake punt that beat Notre Dame at Spartan Stadium, and to this day doctors aren't completely certain why something so unlikely happened to a man so otherwise healthy.

He was always a fairly healthy eater, big on fish and chicken. His weight was good. His cholesterol low. But he had a mild cardiac ambush that knocked him from the sidelines for a couple of weeks. And his lifestyle, if anything, has become even more disciplined in the days since.

He exercises 20-30 minutes five or so days a week, either running or weightlifting or riding a stationary bike. He gets his sleep, knowing the biggest enemy to health and to clear thinking is a weary mind and body.

He will watch a movie with Becky, "CIA-type stuff," being his preference. He likes books of a similar genre: "Unbroken," the classic by Laura Hillenbrand, or "Lone Survivor," the heart-pounding account of the Navy SEALS operation that dispatched Osama bin Laden.

And then there is the usual coach's array of self-help books he digests for insights and comparisons. And that's sort of ironic, in an amusing sense, the idea a coach would look to himself, principally, for help.

He runs a football team, after all.

And maybe, in Michigan State's case if Saturday night goes East Lansing's way, it will be a championship team.

Then you get it. Self-help is another term for preparing for peace. Do your best. Play your best. Live with the results. The guy in the sweat pants and Nike shirt is comfortable with his and his team's fate.

Mark Dantonio led MSU to its first undefeated Big Ten season since 1966.

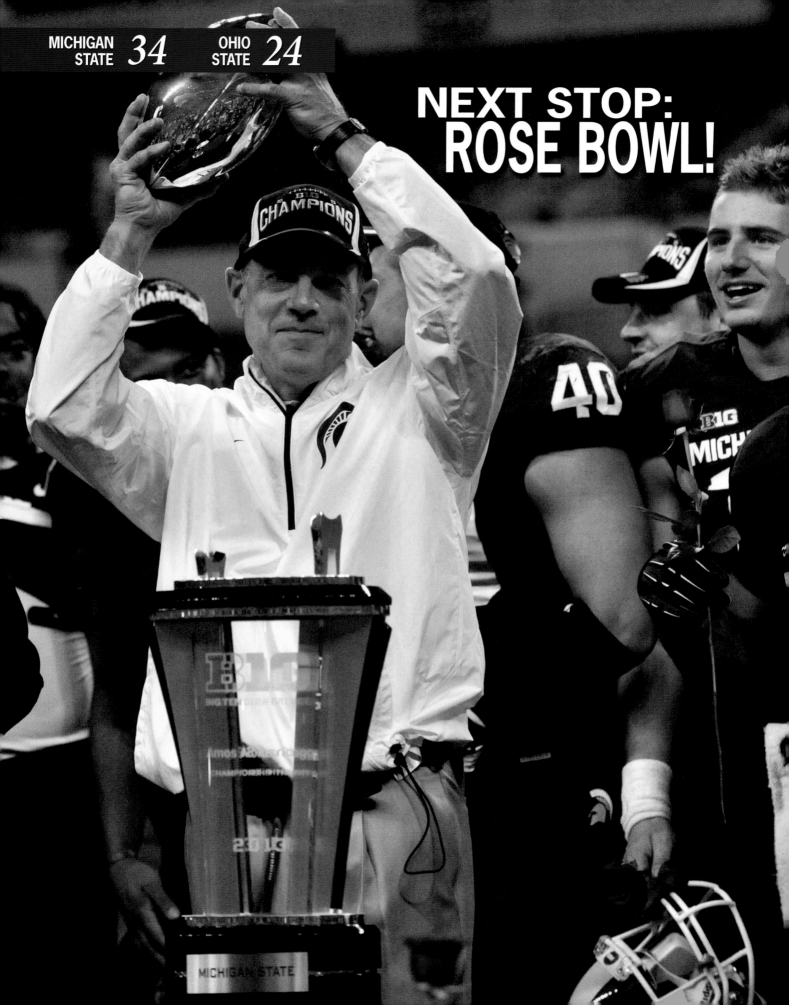

MICHIGAN STATE **34**   OHIO STATE **24**

NEXT STOP: ROSE BOWL!

Michigan State 34, Ohio State 24

Michigan State knocks off Ohio State for Big Ten title, Rose Bowl berth

Saturday, December 7, 2013 | Indianapolis

Story by Matt Charboneau | Photos by Dale G. Young

Indianapolis — The confetti flew from the ceiling of Lucas Oil Field on Saturday night and Michigan State players clutched roses in their hands, not wanting to let go like they might wake up from a dream if they did.

Coaches stood to the side, smiles from ear to ear, watching the men they had pushed and prodded ever since the Spartans finished last season at 7-6 and their head coach told them they would be the team to get Michigan State back to the Rose Bowl.

R.J. Shelton sprints downfield, leaving sprawling Buckeyes defenders behind.

Michigan State 34, Ohio State 24

Coach Mark Dantonio proudly smiles as Connor Cook hoists the Big Ten championship trophy.

No. 10 Michigan State had just done what many believed impossible nearly 12 months ago, even just four months ago when the 2013 season started. The Spartans defeated No. 2 Ohio State, 34-24, in front of a Big Ten championship-record crowd of 66,002 to lock up the team's first trip to the Rose Bowl since Jan. 1, 1988. MSU will face Stanford, which captured the Pac-12 title on Saturday by beating Arizona State.

"I never get too excited; I never get too down," coach Mark Dantonio said. "I live for my players. Our players, I'm so happy for them. They made a lifetime moment tonight for all of us. All of us had that moment, our fans, our players. It will be a moment that we'll never forget."

It was a moment few outside of East Lansing believed that would become reality, and midway through the third quarter on Sat-

Michigan State 34, Ohio State 24

Keith Mumphery scored the game's first touchdown on a pass from Connor Cook.

Michigan State 34, Ohio State 24

Denicos Allen (28) and Trae Waynes (15) bring down Buckeyes QB Braxton Miller.

urday night against an Ohio State team that had won 24 straight games, it seemed just as far-fetched.

But that's when a defense that had been gouged for better than 130 yards rushing in just one quarter stiffened and the offense — one so maligned early in the season — came to life, much like it had early in the game. Trailing 24-17, the Spartans marched 90 yards to take the lead early in the fourth quarter on

a 9-yard touchdown pass from Connor Cook to Josiah Price.

And then, after a huge fourth-down stop on defense, the Spartans put the finishing touches on the victory when Jeremy Langford raced 26 yards for the final touchdown.

"That's what we do," said Langford, who gained 128 yards on 24 carries. "Finish the game the right way. The offensive line did a great job of blocking once again and we fin-

Michigan State 34, Ohio State 24

Jeremy Langford (33) gained 128 yards on 24 carries for the Spartans.

ished it the right way and we're headed to the Rose Bowl."

The right way came after some pretty significant swings in momentum.

The Spartans, who won 12 games for the first time in program history, scored the first 17 points of the game and looked like they would be cruising to Pasadena.

The opening drive of the game lasted 14 plays and took 6:29 off the clock as Michigan State took a 3-0 lead on a 40-yard field goal from Michael Geiger. The drive was aided by a pair of pass interference calls on the Buck-

eyes, both of which came on third down.

Michigan State struck again on the first play of the second quarter as Connor Cook connected with Keith Mumphery on a 72-yard touchdown pass to put the Spartans up 10-0 with just 10 seconds gone. Ohio State defensive back Corey Brown took a bad angle and tried to go for the ball as Cook threw a perfect strike. The Spartans kept pouring it on midway through the second quarter as Cook hit Tony Lippett in stride with a 33-yard touchdown pass to give the Spartans a 17-0 lead with 9:01 left in the half.

Michigan State 34, Ohio State 24

Max Bullough, left, and Denicos Allen are drenched in confetti in Indianapolis.

But Ohio State finally got its offense going and answered quickly with its most impressive drive of the game, sparked by a 48-yard run by quarterback Braxton Miller, who appeared as if he would be sacked but got loose for the big gain. Miller finished the drive with a 20-yard strike to Corey Brown to cut the Michigan State lead to 17-7 with just more than six minutes left in the first half.

Ohio State tacked on a 28-yard field goal

Michigan State 34, Ohio State 24

by Drew Basil on the final play of the half to cut Michigan State's lead to 17-10 as Miller accounted for 161 of Ohio State's 198 yards in the first half. The Buckeyes kept the momentum rolling in the second half, taking the opening kick and going 75 yards in 2:39 to tie the game at 17 with 12:21 left in the third quarter. Miller scored on an 8-yard run as Ohio State completed just one pass on the drive, pounding away at Michigan State on the ground.

After a punt by the Spartans, Ohio State kept hammering Michigan State on the ground, taking the lead on a 6-yard run by

Miller to take its first lead at 24-17.

"We opened it up a little bit, let Braxton throw the ball," Ohio State coach Urban Meyer said. "Did a nice job at the end of the half to get down there, kick a field goal. We also did a nice job making some adjustments by alignments with receivers to give us advantages in the run game. ... The best thing was our defense really played well for about three or four series there and we were able to take the lead."

In the third quarter alone, Ohio State ran for 137 yards. It was quite a surprise against a Michigan State defense that entered the game as the No. 1 defense in the nation, allowing less than 65 yards a game on the ground.

In fact, the Spartans had allowed only two 100-yard rushers all season and Miller (142) and Hyde (118) were both over that number in three quarters.

"There was a moment when they took the energy out of our defense," linebacker Max Bullough said. "We needed to get our swag back, whether that was the offense having a long drive or us making a big play."

Denicos Allen (28) and Darqueze Dennard (31) stop OSU QB Braxton Miller in his tracks.

Michigan State 34, Ohio State 24

Isaiah Lewis (9) brings down OSU QB Braxton Miller.

It turns out the Spartans got both.

First, Michigan State stopped the string of 24 straight from the Buckeyes with 2:29 to play in the third quarter when Geiger connected on a 44-yard field goal to cut the Ohio State lead to 24-20. Then the Spartans got a crucial stop on defense and the offense came to life to grab the lead back. They went 90 yards on eight plays to recapture a 27-24 lead on a 9-yard pass from Cook to Price with 11:41 to play in the game.

The Spartans defense had one more big play left as Ohio State faced a fourth-and-two at the Michigan 39 with 5:46 to play. Miller tried to run to the outside, but Michigan State linebacker Denicos Allen dragged him down for a 1-yard gain and the Spartans took over.

Six plays later, Langford then capped the game with his final touchdown run and sent Michigan State — finally — back to Pasadena.

"This is a football team," Dantonio said. "We weren't ranked in the top 25 until sometime the end of October. So this is a football team that's earned its way. We've not backed into any games. We didn't back into this championship game. We're not backing in to the Rose Bowl. We're going the right way."

They're going as Big Ten champions.

Michigan State 34, Ohio State 24

MSU QB Connor Cook (18) was named MVP of the Big Ten Championship Game.

Michigan State 34, Ohio State 24

Michigan State rises to the occasion, top of Big Ten

By Bob Wojnowski

MSU defensive coordinator Pat Narduzzi, left, embraces head coach Mark Dantonio.

Michigan State 34, Ohio State 24

Indianapolis — This is what they do, hit and hit and hit again. And then, just when you think they're running out of swings, they hit even harder.

The Spartans just hit it big, as big as imaginable. They kicked in the long-locked door and kicked aside history, and did it the way they've done it all year. Their top-ranked defense rebounded when it had to and their underrated quarterback rose to the moment, and on a remarkable Saturday night, the Spar-

tans finally rose to the Roses.

This was punishing, then puzzling, then right back to punishing, as Michigan State slapped Ohio State, 34-24, to win the Big Ten title. The Spartans posted a school-record 12th victory and snapped the Buckeyes' 24-game winning streak, and denied them a spot in the BCS championship game.

This isn't about Ohio State being exposed (which it was). This is about Michigan State's program under Mark Dantonio being na-

Buckeyes QB Braxton Miller scrambles to recover a fumble as Max Bullough (40) and Ed Davis (43) bring him down for a significant loss of yardage.

Michigan State 34, Ohio State 24

tionally revealed, reaching about the highest point possible. On the field of Lucas Oil Stadium, rose stems and petals were scattered among the confetti as the Spartans stood toward their cheering fans and belted out the fight song. The long hunt and the long haunt are over, as Michigan State grabbed its first Rose Bowl bid in 26 years.

If it felt like a cleansing for Spartans fans, well, that's pretty much how it felt for the players and coaches.

Keith Mumphery sprints downfield while Buckeyes coach Urban Meyer, left, looks on.

"This is legendary," said linebacker Denicos Allen, who made the crucial fourth-down stop. "We're going down in history. Whenever they talk about the last Michigan State Rose Bowl team, they're gonna talk about us now. That's legendary to me, because we've been talking about the last Rose Bowl team forever."

By vanquishing the Buckeyes, the Spartans actually did the SEC a favor, allowing Auburn to play Florida State for the BCS championship. Michigan State will face Stanford in the Rose Bowl, and that might be a matchup of the two toughest teams in America.

How tough? The Spartans jumped to a 17-0 lead but couldn't contain Braxton Mill-

er and Carlos Hyde, and the Buckeyes rolled back with 24 straight points. It looked like a major buckling and it was, then it wasn't, and that's how these resilient Spartans roll. Defensive coordinator Pat Narduzzi came charging down from the press box in the third quarter and joined the team on the sideline, something he seldom does. Michigan State's defense needed a kick, and it got a huge one.

With the Spartans leading 27-24 and only 5:46 remaining, the Buckeyes faced a fourth-and-two from the Michigan State 39. The way the Spartans were moving the ball behind the passing of Connor Cook, Urban Meyer figured he had to go for it. Miller rolled right

Michigan State 34, Ohio State 24

and was met squarely by Allen, who stuffed him a yard shy of the first down.

How tough? For all the wild runs by Miller (142 yards) and Hyde (118), Ohio State was only 1-for-10 on third-down conversions and 0-for-2 on fourth downs.

"We stayed the course," Dantonio said. "Again, pretty much like it's been all season long — we just sort of battle, battle, battle."

They battle and they gamble, and that faith between the coaches and players is the bedrock of this rock-solid team. Dantonio tried an onside kick in the fourth quarter after taking the 27-24 lead and it nearly worked. Narduzzi still blitzed plenty, then adjusted as Miller and Hyde plowed up the middle. By the time underrated Jeremy Langford clinched it on a 26-yard touchdown run with 2:16 left, the Buckeyes already were beaten.

"It's going to haunt all of us, I imagine, for a little while, but that's part of the game," Meyer said. "We got to do things a little bit better. I don't want to take anything away from our opponent, because that's a heck of a team, man. Good players, good scheme."

Michigan State was 9-0 against Big Ten opponents, all nine victories by double digits. That's amazing, and this was an amazingly topsy-turvy game.

The stands were filled with about 70 percent Buckeyes fans, so the Spartans again were outnumbered and outflanked. But they never, ever are outworked or out-toughed. In fact, when they hit back after losing the lead, the Buckeyes were staggered. Their receivers dropped passes, their secondary was horrible, and in the end, they couldn't stop Cook, who was 24-for-40 for 304 yards.

As absolutions go, this was thorough. The Spartans snatched back a game the Buckeyes had appeared to snatch, and gobbled all sorts

of redemption. Safety Isaiah Lewis was back in his hometown trying to forever shake the memory of his penalty two years ago that sealed the loss to Wisconsin. This time, he was terrific, and led the Spartans with 13 tackles.

"I'm on top of the world right now," Lewis said. "This is even better than I thought, way better than I thought. Coach (Narduzzi) had to hype us up and remind us we're the No. 1 defense in the country, so just keep playing and doing your thing."

Their thing is to hit as hard as possible as often as possible. And their other thing these days is to dance as wildly as possible afterward.

In the Michigan State dressing room, the rap music blared and players took turns bounding into the middle of the fray, singing along to make the sweetest noise ever. Off to the side, senior linebacker Max Bullough stood in full uniform, and just shook his head.

"I do feel cleansed," he said. "Now I can watch TV, I can watch ESPN, I can watch the Big Ten Network, and they can say whatever they want. We won. We did it. No if's, no buts, no we didn't play someone. We did it. There's nothing you can say anymore."

The only thing left to say is what the Spartans have craved to hear, and earned the right to hear. They're the best in the Big Ten, the toughest team around, no more questions asked.

MICHIGAN STATE 24   STANFORD 20

ROSES ARE
GREEN

Michigan State 24, Stanford 20

Green day: Michigan State is Rose Bowl champion once again

Wednesday, January 1, 2014 | Pasadena, California
Story by Matt Charboneau | Photos by Dale G. Young

Pasadena, Calif. — The 26-year wait seemed like nothing on Wednesday night.

Michigan State was the Rose Bowl champion once again.

In its first appearance in the game since 1988, No. 4 Michigan State defeated No. 5 Stanford, 24-20, in front of a pro-MSU crowd of 95,173 in the 100th playing of the Rose Bowl.

The Spartans (13-1) got 332 yards passing from Connor Cook and a huge fourth-down stop in the final minutes to secure the victory.

Clinging to the four-point lead, Michigan State needed to hold Stanford on fourth-and-1 from the Stanford 34 and just 1:45 left on the clock.

That's when fifth-year senior linebacker Kyler Elsworth, in for the suspended Max

Stanford's Ty Montgomery gets tackled by MSU's Isiah Lewis (9) and Kyler Elsworth (47).

Darqueze Dennard(31) leads the Spartans as they warm-up at the Rose Bowl.

Bullough, soared over the pile and stuck Stanford fullback Ryan Hewitt to turn the ball over and seal the victory for the Spartans.

Jeremy Langford ran for 84 yards and a touchdown for the Spartans while Tony Lippett caught five passes for 94 yards and a touchdown.

Stanford (11-3) said it was going to take shots downfield and did so on the second

play of the game as Kevin Hogan hit Michael Rector for a 43-yard gain that set the Cardinal up deep in Michigan State territory.

The Cardinal capitalized with a 16-yard run by Tyler Gaffney that gave them an early 7-0 lead less than five minutes into the game.

The big plays continued to hurt Michigan State as Stanford got a 47-yard run from Gaffney on the opening play of a seven-play drive

and went up 10-0 on a 34-yard field goal from Jordan Williamson.

The Spartans had a chance to make a big play when Stanford quarterback Kevin Hogan fumbled the ball and several Spartans had a shot to recover. They failed to come up with the ball, however, and the Cardinal extended their lead late in the first quarter.

Michigan State got right back in the game early in the second quarter with a 13-play, 75-yard drive that ended with a 2-yard touch-down run by Langford.

The Spartans took advantage when Stanford was called for pass interference in the end zone on third-and-goal from the 9-yard line as Cook tried to complete a pass in the end zone to Macgarrett Kings Jr.

But just as Michigan State was starting to gain some momentum, Cook made his biggest mistake of the season, throwing an interception that was returned 40 yards for a touchdown by Stanford linebacker Kevin An-

Michigan State 24, Stanford 20

derson. It was redemption for Anderson who earlier dropped a potential interception.

Cook was trying to set up a screen to Langford but never saw Anderson, who was untouched on his way to the end zone.

But Cook and the Spartans responded in the final two minutes of the half and cut the Stanford lead back to three points. Cook hit Bennie Fowler for 34 yards then found fullback Trevon Pendleton for a 2-yard touchdown pass with 28 seconds left in the first half to cut Stanford's lead to 17-14 with 28 seconds left in the first half.

Michigan State took the opening kick of the second half and went 61 yards on six plays to tie the game at 17 on a 31-yard field goal by Michael Geiger. Cook hit Fowler with a 60-yard pass on the second play of the half, but the drive stalled after a first-down sack and the Spartans had to settle for three points.

Michigan State took its first lead of the game just minutes into the fourth quarter when Cook avoided the Stanford blitz and hit Tony Lippett with a 24-yard touchdown pass to give the Spartans a 24-17 lead with 13:22 to play in the game.

The Spartans began the drive at the Car-

Michigan State defenders upend Stanford quarterback Kevin Hogan and force a fumble.

dinal 27 when the defense stuffed the Stanford offense inside its own 10 and Macgarrett Kings Jr. returned the ensuing punt 19 yards.

After Michigan State was forced to punt, Stanford took over with 9:01 to play from its 28 and immediately got into Spartans territo-

Michigan State 24, Stanford 20

Stanford caught a huge break when referees ruled this tackle of Tyler Gaffney in the end zone was NOT a safety.

ry on a 27-yard run from Michael Rector on a reverse and then took advantage of a defensive holding penalty on Darqueze Dennard.

On third-and-6 from the MSU 29, Hogan picked up enough to get the first down and keep the drive moving. But Denzel Drone came up with a big sack on second down to push the Cardinal back to the 28 and Michigan State held to force a field-goal attempt

Stanford avoided disaster on a botched snap on a field goal when they completed a first-down pass but were flagged for an in-

Michigan State 24, Stanford 20

eligible receiver downfield. The penalty gave the Cardinal another shot and Jordan Williamson connected from 39 yards to cut Michigan State's lead to 24-20 with 4:15 to play in the fourth quarter.

After the Spartans got the ball back, Langford carried two straight times for nothing and the Spartans faced a third-and-11 with 3:24 to play only to have a pass knocked down and be forced to punt.

Stanford took over at its 25 with 3:06 to play and one timeout left but couldn't convert a first down as the Spartans stuffed the Cardinal on fourth down.

Michigan State quarterback Connor Cook throws a first down pass.

Michigan State 24, Stanford 20

MSU's Tony Lippett dives over Stanford's Wayne Lyons for the go ahead touchdown.

BOX SCORE

	1	2	3	4	T
#5 STANFORD	10	7	0	3	20
#4 MSU	0	14	3	7	24

SCORING SUMMARY

FIRST QUARTER

STAN: TD 11:16 Tyler Gaffney 16 Yd Run (Jordan Williamson Kick)

FG 01:40 Jordan Williamson 34 Yd

SECOND QUARTER

MSU: TD 10:45 Jeremy Langford 2 Yd Run (Michael Geiger Kick)

STAN: TD 02:07 Kevin Anderson 40 Yd Interception Return (Jordan Williamson Kick)

MSU: TD 00:28 Trevon Pendleton 2 Yd Pass From Connor Cook (Michael Geiger Kick)

THIRD QUARTER

MSU: FG 12:56 Michael Geiger 31 Yd

FOURTH QUARTER

MSU: TD 13:22 Tony Lippett 25 Yd Pass From Connor Cook (Michael Geiger Kick)

STAN: FG 04:15 Jordan Williamson 39 Yd

MSU's Jeremy Langford celebrates his touchdown with teammate Fou Fonoti.

Michigan State 24, Stanford 20

Coach Dantonio celebrates with Macgarrett Kings, Jr. as MSU beats Stanford, 24-20.

MSU's Denzel Drone celebrates as his team stopped Stanford's final drive.

Connor Cook walks off the field after MSU beats Stanford, 24-20, in the 100th Tournament of Roses.